ALL YOU EVER NEED IS JESUS

REV. JERRY C. CROSSLEY

Copyright ©2025 by Rev. Jerry C. Crossley (Higher Ground Books & Media)
All rights reserved. No part of this publication may be reproduced in any form, stored in a retrieval system, or transmitted in any form, or by any means (electronic, mechanical, photocopying, recording or otherwise) without prior permission by the copyright owner and the publisher of this book.

Scripture taken from the HOLY BIBLE, NEW INTERNATIONAL VERSION® NIV®. Copyright © 1973, 1978, 1984 by International Bible Society. Used by permission of Zondervan. All rights reserved worldwide.

Higher Ground Books & Media
Springfield, OH 45504
www.highergroundbooksandmedia.com

Because of the dynamic nature of the Internet, any web addresses or links contained in this book may have changed since publication and may no longer be valid. The views expressed in the work are solely those of the author and do not necessarily reflect the views of the publisher, and the publisher hereby disclaims any responsibility for them.

Any people depicted in stock imagery are being used for illustrative purposes only.

ISBN (Paperback): 978-1-955368-97-1

Printed in the United States of America 2025

ALL YOU EVER NEED IS JESUS

REV. JERRY C. CROSSLEY

ACKNOWLEDGEMENTS

1. Of course, my perennial typist, Dan Keen, who handles all the nitty gritty of manuscript preparation. His own kindness and gentleness defines what a Christian should be.

2. My readers. Many people have privately assured me that reading books is passé. "People don't read today. Nobody finds that books are relevant." Maybe my next book will have no words, only emojis.

3. The members of the congregations we serve, past and present. All of us are imperfect people, but each of us hopefully finds ourselves "in the same boat" as we voyage through life. That boat is our faith community. That boat, by the grace of God, becomes the Ark of our salvation.

All You Ever Need Is Jesus is a devotional commentary based on St. Paul's pastoral letter to the Colossians.

Introduction

The little Christian community in the city of Colossae was in turmoil. The new-found faith they cherished was under a subtle attack by those who denigrated the Gospel and wanted to substitute some other way of salvation. At this critical juncture, the Apostle Paul wrote a heart-felt pastoral letter to counter the apostasy. He probably wrote from prison somewhere around A.D. 62[1]. He made his appeal to these Christians in Colossae, a once-prosperous small town in what, today, would be Western Turkey[2].

In exploring the cultural, historical, theological background of Paul's letter, it dawned on me that he was reacting against a whole range of heresies: Gnosticism, asceticism, legalism, angel worship, mystery cults, libertinism. All of them contended for the loyalty of the believer. One scholar pointed out that there were those Christians who would happily add strange philosophies to the Gospel, just like tossing more ingredients into a stew. They failed to grasp the truth that the Gospel stands complete in itself, and that Jesus alone is God's answer[3]. We don't "mix and match".

The Colossians were interested in adding onto their faith, like something was somehow missing! It wasn't enough that they had found Christ, or that He had found them. They thought they needed something more, or something different. There's a little story about a farmer who always fed his mule expensive oats. In a cost-saving gambit, he decided to gradually substitute sawdust for oats in the mule's diet. Now it took a little while for the animal to become accustomed to the change in its feed, but just about the time he got used to the substitute, he died. That's what can happen to your own spiritual life. The switch from gospel truth to biblical error might be a slow and subtle transition (like feed to sawdust). The average Christian consumer isn't even aware of it. Then suddenly he's dead![4]

Once Paul had written to the Christians in the Greek city of Corinth, "Now, brothers, I want to remind you of the gospel I preached to you, which you received and on which you have taken your stand. By this gospel you are saved, if you hold firmly to the word I have preached to you."[5] Your decision can be a life-or-death choice. Somewhere I once read these words: "In the Person of Jesus Christ there is a Way of Life that abounds in steadfast love; there is Truth - simple, unchanging, and redeeming; and there is Life - with power, purpose, and fulfillment."

The main message of Colossians is that Jesus is all you need[6]. So I have entitled this book All You Ever Need - - - Is Jesus. In his book, Our Sufficiency in Christ, John MacArthur, Jr. told about an evangelist who had been invited to preach at a cluster of churches. One family, whose home was centrally located, offered to host him. After a preaching service, he returned, late at night, to the home of his hosts. The weather was freezing cold; the wind, blustery. As he approached the home, he could see that the lights were on. Yet nobody answered when he stood there, knocking on the door. He could not arouse the family inside. He thought about knocking on a neighbor's door and asking if he could use their phone to contact his hosts. Then he thought better of it. After all, a stranger knocking, late at night, on someone's front door might panic the occupant.

At that point, he decided to walk to a public phone and make the call. Trouble is that he didn't know where one was. So he trudged through the bitter cold until he finally observed the neon lights of a motel and made his phone call. "I'm sorry to wake you up, but I stood outside knocking on your front door, and nobody answered."

A tired voice said, "My friend, look in your pocket. Don't you remember that, before you left my house, I gave you the front door key?" Embarrassed, the evangelist searched his pockets and found the key. John MacArthur concluded that too many Christians are looking in too many places for blessings, when - all the time - each Christian happens to be holding the key to abundant and eternal life. The key is Jesus himself. You don't need to look anywhere else[7]. All you ever need is Jesus!

Chapter 1: "Grace and Peace to You" (Colossians 1:2 NIV)

At the opening of his letter, Paul used two really magical words, "grace" and "peace". Grace is a word that describes the free, unmerited gift of God's love. There are times when we feel that we cannot love ourselves, let alone anyone else. Then comes the awareness that God loves us – not because of who we are but in spite of who we are. I will never forget the night when, as a 22 year-old, I had experienced complete despair. I cried to the Lord, "Please, God if You are here, and if You even care, deliver me from my despondency. Forgive me for my incorrigible self-centeredness. Thank You for dying on the cross for me. (I wasn't sure what that meant). I can't manage my life anymore. Please come into my heart and by my Lord and Savior. Place my life under new management."

That was my prayer: simple, sincere, and an act of self-surrender. My whole room seemed to light up supernaturally, and I experienced - in a word - acceptance. I had stepped into the experience of Grace. This gift of God's love is not confined to one climactic moment at the beginning of our faith-walk; it's an ongoing encounter with His all-pervading love. God's grace will accompany you every step of your pilgrimage.

A man named John Newton lived a very rough life in the 18th century and became a slave-trader[1]. He was bad-tempered and profane. Then when he finally surrendered himself to the Lord, he experienced a flood of God's grace. At the end of his life he wrote, "My memory is nearly gone, but I remember two things, that I am a great sinner, and that Christ is a great Savior."[2] His tombstone reads: "John Newton, -- Once An Infidel And Libertine --- Was By the Rich Mercy of Our Lord And Savior Jesus Christ Preserved, Restored, Pardoned, and Appointed to Preach The Faith He Had Long Labored To Destroy."[3]

With a humble recognition that we can know God's grace each step of the way. John Newton was moved to write the words of his most famous hymn (in fact, perhaps the most famous hymn in all of Christendom): "Amazing grace - how sweet the sound - /That saved a wretch like me! /I once was lost by now am found, /Was blind but now I see. //'Twas grace that taught my heart to fear,/ And grace my fears relieved; /How precious did that grace appear, /The hour I first believed!// Through many dangers, toils and snares/ I have already come; /'Tis grace hath brought me safe thus far, /And grace will lead me Home[4]."

"Grace and Peace to you[5]." See the arrangement of these two words? Paul did not write "Peace and grace" but "Grace and peace." That's not accidental. For until we experience God's grace, we can never know His peace[6]. God's peace is made possible by His grace[7]. I don't imagine that you are going to enjoy His peace until, and unless, you invite Him into your life.

I will never forget the time that a young woman came forward to the altar rail at the conclusion of a worship service. Her whole life was in disarray, mostly because of wrong choices she had made. I never wanted to intrude if congregants wanted to pray privately without sharing their prayer. Yet this woman seemed so desperate that I knelt beside her and asked if I might pray for her. "Oh yes, please," she said. "What do you want me to pray for?" "I just want to pray for God's peace," she whimpered.

"Did you ever invite Jesus into your life?" I inquired. "No," she answered, angrily and emphatically. "Well, would you like to? We can pray together right here." She bristled defensively and said, "What is this? Some sort of a package deal?" Momentarily stunned by her attack, I was at first hesitant to say anything at all, afraid to "upset the apple cart." Then I marshalled my resources and replied, "Yes, you got that right. It's exactly what it is: a 'package deal'. For Jesus is our peace. Without Him, you can never know real peace." She stood up and furiously stomped away from the altar, away from the commitment, away from authentic and abundant life, away from Jesus.

In his letter to the Philippians, Paul wrote, "And the peace of God, which transcends all understanding, will guard your hearts and your minds in Christ Jesus."[8] I have noticed that whenever we use the word "peace" we have a tendency to couple it with the word "quiet" as in "All I want is a little peace and quiet." So, in our mind, peace is related to an absence of worry, of frenetic activity, of turmoil and conflict. But "peace" in the Bible means more than an absence; it indicates the positive presence of God's love. Ernest Martin states that it means the presence of a total well-being, something that comes only as a gift from God[9].

A Sunday School class of little children was being shown a picture of a storm on the Sea of Galilee. A fishing boat was nearly capsizing amidst the turbulence of the wind and the broiling waves of the sea. Jesus and His disciples were in that hapless, hopeless boat. One of the little boys commented, "That's really a scary storm. I'm sure glad I wasn't in that boat!" At that, a little girl in the class countered, "I wish I were with them in that boat." The Sunday School teacher was a little surprised and asked, "Why? Why would you like to have been there in that big storm?" She answered, very ingenuously, "Because Jesus was there with them!"[10]

Chapter 2: "We Have Heard of Your Faith --- and ---Love" (Col.1:4 NIV)

In his loneliness, Paul was grateful that God surrounded him with fellow Christians. The Apostle prayed for them, and they prayed, in turn, for him. They were his brothers and sisters in the Lord. He wrote, "...We have heard of your faith in Christ Jesus..." [1] A missionary, John G. Paton, was attempting to translate the Bible into the language of an indigenous people. He was completely stonewalled when he discovered that they had no word for "faith". At last he hit upon the phrase "to lean your whole weight upon." That's what faith in the Lord really amounts to: We lean our whole weight on Him[2].

Many people preach the necessity of having faith, and it doesn't matter what or whom you have faith in. As long as you have Faith! So they continuously champion the efficacy of having faith in faith. However, the Christian doesn't have faith in faith; the Christian has faith in Christ. So Paul wrote, "We have heard of your faith in Christ Jesus..."[3]

Clarence Macartney recalled the story of a woman who visited him once for some counseling. She sat there and rattled off a whole laundry list of all the trials she had faced and crushing sorrows and defeats she had endured. Finally, she summarized the whole tragic story by exclaiming, "Oh, if I had not had the advantage of knowing Jesus!" That's all she said, or all she had to say. Immediately, the pastor understood. Macartney ended his narrative by asking the reader, "What does this Jesus mean to you? Who is He for you? Do you know Him as your hope for today? Do you know Him as your hope for eternity? Are you able to say with this woman, 'Oh, if I had not known Him!'?"[4]

The Apostle Paul wrote to the Colossians, "... We have heard of your faith in Christ Jesus and of the love you have for all the saints..."[5] People in our culture are always talking about "love" and singing about "love". But they persist in viewing it primarily as a feeling. You feel "in love". Love is something you fall into. "Last night I fell in love." It sounds so sweet, but it's a distortion. The truth of the matter is that love is much more than a feeling, depending on your hormones or your digestive tract. Love is a set will. Love is more than something you simply feel; it's something you do.

On the night of the Last Supper, Jesus said, "A new command I give you: Love one another. As I have loved you, so must you love one another. By this all men will know that you are my disciples, if you love one another."[6] When Jesus spoke of love He wasn't talking about a sticky sweet sentimental feeling, but a larger love based on a relentless good will.[7] The ensuing episode of the foot-washing demonstrates what this love looks like. The disciples were reclining around the table. Their sandaled feet were mud-caked. A servant should have performed the customary washing of the feet of the invited guests.

But no servant was there. Where was the servant? The tricky answer was that they were all the servants. Jesus was, and is, calling each of His followers to be servants. On that same night "a dispute arose among them as to which of them was considered to be the greatest. Jesus said to them, "The kings of the Gentiles lord it over them; and those who exercise authority over them call themselves Benefactors. But you are not to be like that. Instead, the greatest among you should be like the youngest, and the one who rules like the one who serves. For who is greater, the one who is at the table or the one who serves? Is it not the one who is at the table? But I am among you as one who serves."[8]

So Jesus got up from the table, stooped down, and washed their feet. Afterwards the would-be followers sat in embarrassed silence. Jesus said, in effect, "Do you see what I just did for you? If I'm not too big to stoop down to you, then you're not too big to stoop down to someone else."[9] Real love sometimes involves forgetting about yourself. The genuinely great person is not the one who struts, but the one who stoops.

Remember what our Lord encountered on another occasion: "But when he saw the crowds, he had compassion on them, because they were harassed and helpless, like sheep without a shepherd."[10] See, that's how Jesus saw them. Others just saw "crowds." Jesus saw persons. He saw persons worth dying for. We must see others not through our eyes, but His.

Paul saluted his brothers and sisters in Colossae,"...because we have heard of your faith in Christ Jesus and of the love you have..."[11] What a wonderful way to be remembered!

Chapter 3: "The Hope That Is Stored Up For You In Heaven" (Col.1:5 NIV)

The Apostle Paul reminded those first Christians in Colossae of "the hope that is stored up for you in heaven."[1] Without any hope we give up; we have lost our sense of direction and purpose. So the Lord God told the Hebrew exiles in Babylon, "'For I know the plans I have for you,' declares the Lord, 'plans to prosper you and not to harm you, plans to give you hope and a future.'"[2] Each of us needs something to look forward to.

William Cowper had nothing to look forward to. Overwhelmed by disappointment and grief, he had sunk to the bottom of the barrel. Feeling utterly hopeless, he decided to end his life. One typically foggy, rainy night in London, he summoned a horse-drawn cab and told the driver to let him out by the London Bridge. He was planning to drop into the Thames River and be done with all life's conflicts. The cabby kept driving - for two hours - finally admitting that he was hopelessly lost in the fog. That's how William Cowper felt. Convinced that he could not do anything right - even kill himself - he decided to make his way on foot. Then, within only about a block, he discovered himself back at his own front door.

In that moment of truth he realized that the Lord's hand was upon his life, and that God had preserved his life for a purpose. He understood that all his hope lay in his relationship with a Savior who cares and who invites us to come into His presence. He sat down and penned those words that, ever since, have supplied hope to perhaps millions[3]:

> "God moves in a mysterious way
> His wonders to perform;
> He plants his footsteps in the sea,
> And rides upon the storm.
>
> "Blind unbelief is sure to err,
> And scan his work in rain;
> God is his own interpreter,
> And he will make it plain."[4]

In 1 Peter we find these words: "Praise be to the God and father of our Lord Jesus Christ! In his great mercy he has given us new birth into a living hope through the resurrection of Jesus Christ from the dead, and into an inheritance that can never perish, spoil or fade - kept in heaven for you..."[5] Those verses suggest to me that you and I, and all who have put their trust in the Lord, have reservations in Heaven. See it in your mind's eye. When we come to the front desk, the clerk will look up and quietly ask, "May I have your name?" He'll page through his Book of Life, look up again and say, "We have your room reserved and have been expecting you."

Corrie ten Boom shared this heart-warming story. She told about a mother who brought her ten-year-old daughter for a consultation with Corrie, a renowned Bible teacher. The mother said, "My daughter faithfully attends Sunday School and wants to become 'a child of God'. Our problem is that she doesn't know how to do it, and neither do I. How shall we proceed?" Corrie considered their problem, then answered, "Let me take her aside for a little talk, just between the two of us."

When they were alone, Corrie said to the young lady, "Look, suppose I wanted to adopt you so that you would be my daughter? Just pretend for a few moments that I really wanted to do that. How could I proceed? Well, I could sign a few legal papers and say, 'That's it. You belong to me now.' But I wouldn't do that to you. Instead I would wait till you said that's what you yourself wanted. Then, I'd ask you, 'Do you like me? Would you like to become my daughter?' If you'd answer that you would very much like to be my child, I would say, 'Then it's already taken care of. I've already prepared for you.'"

At this point Corrie said the her, "And that's just how you become a child of God. He is patiently waiting to see if that's what you really want to do, and if, in prayer, you tell Him 'Yes,' He will say, 'Then it's all taken care of. I have been expecting you and have already prepared for you.'" Corrie read a passage from the Bible (John 1:12), and then the two of them knelt in prayer. The young girl asked the Lord to make her His child.[6]

She found the hope of Heaven in her heart. The blind poet Fanny Crosby wrote:

> "All the way my Savior leads me;
> O the fullness of his love!
> Perfect rest to me is promised
> In my Father's house above.
> When my spirit, clothed immortal,
> Wings its flight to realms of day,
> This my song through endless ages:
> Jesus led me all the way..."[7]

Chapter 4: "Bearing Fruit And Growing" (Col. 1:6 NIV)

Paul was assessing the progress of the Good News when he wrote, "All over the world this gospel is bearing fruit and growing..."[1] When Simon Peter blurted out, "You are the Christ, the Son of the living God," Jesus responded, "Blessed are you, Simon son of Jonah, for this was not revealed to you by man, but by my Father in heaven. And I tell you that you are Peter, and on this rock I will build my church, and the gates of Hell will not overcome it."[2]

Now all of us know that a gate is a defensive weapon. It's definitely not an offensive weapon. I mean, picture a battlefield where soldiers are advancing, each one swinging a gate. No, gates are used - no pun intended - for defense. So when Jesus is describing "the gates of Hell (or Hades)," he's describing Hell on the defensive. Why? Because Christ's Church is on the offense. And whenever it is, it will triumph. Then it will bear fruit, the light of the gospel will grow, and its illumination will spread across this dark world.

The world is God's target. "For God so loved the world"![3] The Apostle Paul's strategy was to establish missionary bases in the key urban areas of the Roman world.[4] So he labored diligently to create Christian centers in Corinth, Philippi, Ephesus: the "big apples" of their day, the transportation and communication hubs of Roman society. So the faith spread. Why? Because it has universal appeal. Anyone, be he a barbarian or the most cultured Greek, could comprehend the simplicity of the gospel and discover the abundant life in Christ.[5] The words, the deeds, the promises of Jesus reach into the deepest recesses of our soul.[6]

Michael P. Green beautifully illustrated the discovery of the grace of God. He told how a seven-year-old boy got separated from this family in Disneyland. When it finally dawned on him that they were no longer with him, he thought he would be able to figure out how to rejoin them. After a long time of futile effort he realized that it was impossible. He had no idea which way to go to find them. There were two things that had to happen. First of all, he had to admit his lostness. And, secondly, someone would have to come and show him the way back. So each of us must recognize our spiritual lostness... And someone then needs to come into our life to show us the way back.[7]

My friend Bruce Heffner took his trumpet and his ardent love for the Lord and went to Romania with Word of Life Mission. Once there, they traveled from town to town, sharing the gospel of Christ Jesus in word and song. Gradually they became aware of the fact that there was one village that was scorned by the rest of the citizenry because it was inhabited by gypsies. "That's where all the gypsies live, and they are really bad people. Don't go there! Those people will steal your wallets, microphones, sound equipment, and everything you have!"

But despite all the warnings and admonitions, Word of Life decided to go there. "...God's word is not chained."[8] Later, Bruce told me it was a scary venture. A large crowed of gypsies surrounded them as they attempted to set up their equipment in the village square. The members of the evangelistic team tried to interpret the mood of the crowd. Were they menacing, or merely curious?

One further problem exacerbating the whole effort was the fact that the witnessing team did not have a bona fide translator with them that day. Instead, they were stuck with a man who could speak only a little Romanian, just enough to get by. Unfortunately, he was not an official translator. But he was all they had.

One of the members of the team proceeded to explain the Biblical plan of salvation. The translator struggled to translate all that into their own language. At the conclusion of the message, the translator invited anyone who wanted to accept Jesus as their personal Lord and Savior to raise their hand. Instantly every hand shot up in the air. The missions team was perplexed." They must have misunderstood what we are trying to say. They're raising their hands without really knowing why. What should we do?"

The team turned to the translator and said, "The gypsies must have misunderstood your words. Explain again to them that plan of salvation. Try to be as clear as possible." So he did that. Once again, the invitation was given; once again every hand rose in response. Once again the team was confused. Just then a rough-looking gypsy shouldered his way through the crowd and said, "You don't have to keep explaining this to us. Everybody understands. We all want to receive Jesus as our Lord and Savior." That day these Christian workers who had been warned not to go there, witnessed an entire village converted to Christ. All because they had been willing to share the Good News!

Chapter 5: "The Knowledge of His Will" (Col. 1:9 NIV)

Remember that, in his pastoral letter to the new Christians in Colossae, Paul was addressing people who, only recently, had been pagans. They had no prior knowledge of the Hebrew Bible or the Septuagint (the Hebrew Bible in Greek) or Moses or the commandments. Now they were followers of Jesus because a man named Epaphras had shared the gospel with them. "You learned it from Epaphras, or dear fellow servant..."[1] He was a citizen of Colossae who had become a Christian and then led his neighbors to the Lord.[2] However, he intentionally left his congregation and came to visit Paul. Epaphras knew that his people needed help. They were being torn apart by heresies and weren't sure what to believe. Paul listened carefully to his friend.[3] Both of them were intent on one thing: that the truth of the Gospel should not be perverted.

Paul's response was this letter. As Ralph Martin described, Epaphras most likely stood at Paul's side while the Apostle composed it.[4] Elsewhere, in the 10th Chapter of Romans, Paul wrote, "For there is no difference between Jew and Gentile - the same Lord is Lord of all and richly blesses all who call on him, for 'Everyone who calls on the name of the Lord will be saved.' How, then, can they call on the one they have not believe in? And how can they believe in the one of whom they have not heard?"[5] Each of us can make Him known. Each of us can be an Epaphras who shares our faith with someone else.

Paul complimented Epaphras for being faithful[6]. Once Jesus poignantly asked, "...when the Son of Man comes, will he find faith on the earth?"[7] In the closing book of the Bible it says, "Be faithful, even to the point of death, and I will give you the crown of life."[8] When the good Lord examines your life, He won't be inquiring if you were popular or successful or famous. He'll be asking only if you were faithful. He won't be asking, "Did you make money?" He'll be asking instead, "Did you make a difference?"

Paul, moved by Epaphras' description of his congregation's turmoil, wrote, "For this reason, since the day we heard about you, we have not stopped praying for you..."[9] I once visited a church member who had been hospitalized with a life-threatening illness.

Jack Lesh was a quiet, gentle man who was a prominent businessman in our community and also an inspiring Sunday School teacher. He said to me, "Last night, as I was lying in bed, I literally felt bathed in prayer." Coincidentally, last night in our prayer meeting, our church members were "storming the gates of Heaven" on behalf of Jack.

Paul continued, "...and asking God to fill you with the knowledge of his will..."[10] The knowledge of His will! That's the task of prayer: to learn God's will. And that is why most of our prayer life should not be speaking but listening.[11] The trouble is that we are so absorbed in following our own will that we don't listen for His. The one question we should be asking is "What is His will for my life?"

One night there was a meeting of the Fellowship of Christian Athletes. Bobby Richardson, a former second baseman on the New York Yankees, was invited to come forward and offer the opening prayer. He surprised everyone with what must have been one of the shortest prayers on record. Yet it went right to the heart of the human heart and probably the heart of God. All he said was, "Dear God, Your will. Nothing more. Nothing less. Nothing else. Amen."[12]

Chapter 6: "Live a Life Worthy of the Lord" (Col. 1:10 NIV)

In the Old Testament, the prophet Micah was wrestling with the question, "How can I live a life worthy of the Lord?" He asked, "With what shall I come before the Lord and bow down before the exalted God? Shall I come before him with burnt offerings, with calves a year old? Will the Lord be pleased with thousands of rams, with ten thousand rivers of oil? Shall I offer my first born for my transgression, the fruit of my body for the sin of my soul? He has showed you, O man, what is good. And what does the Lord require of you? To act justly and to love mercy and to walk humbly with your God."[1]

Centuries later the Apostle Paul expressed his own highest hopes for the followers of Jesus: "And we pray...that you may live a life worthy of the Lord..."[2] In the preceding verse Paul had prayed that his brothers and sisters in Christ might be filled "with the knowledge of his will."[3] Why is it so important to know God's will for your life? So that you may walk worthy of Him.[4] To the Christians in the church at Ephesus St. Paul had written, "As a prisoner for the Lord, then, I urge you to live a life worthy of the calling you have received."[5]

It should be obvious to you that just knowing the Lord's will isn't enough; you have to follow it. Just knowing that God wants you to follow a certain path is not sufficient; you have to walk it.[6] A great preacher, Charles Haddon Spurgeon, once remarked that everything has a specific, God-given purpose in life, and that God has a purpose for everyone. The Lord did not create anyone to be just a cipher, a zero, a nonentity. Therefore, your spiritual task is to discover God's purpose and then pursue it.[7]

Paul's further prayer and hope was that you and I and those Colossians "may please him in every way."[8] Generally we mortals labor to please everyone else around us, because we want them to love and accept us. Often we don't think at all about pleasing God. So we consequently make bad decisions. Paul saw fit to reverse this when he wrote to the sisters and brother in Galatia, "Am I now trying to win the approval of men, or of God? Or am I trying to please men? If I were still trying to please men, I would not be a servant of Christ."[9]

Too many of us Christians are like an old man (I am an old man already!) who was trudging along with his donkey and his grandson. He was leading his donkey while his grandson walked behind them. They came to a village, and the villagers, watching this scene, freely offered their critique: "Old man, why are you so foolishly leading the donkey and walking ahead of it? Why aren't you riding him?" So, just to please them, he took their advice and mounted the donkey.

When a whole new crowd of people, in the next village, saw the old man riding the donkey while his little grandson walked behind, they said, "You're cruel and selfish, making that little boy walk while you just sit there on the donkey!" So, just to please them, he dismounted and placed his grandson on the donkey. But when they arrived at the third village, the curious onlookers said, "Little boy, you are lazy and thoughtless, making this old man walk while you just sit there on that donkey. Both of you should get on the donkey and ride him." So, just to please them, the old man did just that.

When the old man, his grandson, and the donkey arrived at the fourth village, the villagers were indignant. "Is this any way to treat a poor donkey? You force him to carry both of you? You should be ashamed of yourself!" The last anyone saw them, the old man and his little grandson were carrying the donkey down the road. That's the confusion that inevitably results when we try to please everybody. We should just work to please God.[10]

Near the conclusion of Hebrews comes this benediction: "May the God of peace, who through the blood of the eternal covenant brought back from the dead our Lord Jesus, that great Shepherd of the sheep, equip you with everything good for doing his will, and may he work in us what is pleasing to him, through Jesus Christ, to whom be glory for ever and ever. Amen."[11]

Paul's highest hope for his Colossians was that "You may live a life worthy of the Lord and may please him in every way: bearing fruit in every good work, growing in the knowledge of God..."[12] The knowledge of God is probably the only knowledge worth having. In the Old Testament book of Jeremiah these words are inscribed: "This is what the Lord says: "Let not the wise man boast of his wisdom, or the strong man boast of his strength or the rich man boast of his riches, but let him who boasts boast about this: that he understands and knows me..."[13]

I have frequently noticed how, in the heat of romantic emotions, many people fall in love with love, instead of in love with a person. Adolescently, they dream and fantasize about their own sublime feelings. By analogy, I share with you the experience of Sammy Tippit. In his insightful book, The Prayer Factor, he described his own spiritual aspiration. As he grew and matured in his faith, he was inspired by the evangelical giants like Dwight L. Moody and Charles Finney. These men had supernatural encounters with God. That's what he wanted. Moody, for instance, was so overwhelmed by God's presence that he prayed that the Lord would back off. And Finney felt that he was being washed in waves of "liquid love". That's the kind of ecstatic encounter that Sammy Tippit was seeking.

But it never happened. He never felt what those other men of God felt, even though he had begged the Lord to favor him with one of those "mountain top" moments. Finally, as he prayed, he realized that he was seeking the wrong thing. It wasn't their experience that he should know; it was their God that he should know[14]. May you also know their Lord and live a life that is worthy of Him.

Chapter 7: "Share in the Inheritance of the Saints" (Col. 1:12 NIV)

Sometimes all of us, despite our professed faith, lose our focus, our resolve, and our courage. Paul also knew that, and so he prayed that each of us may be "strengthened with all power according to his glorious might..."[1] To the Christians in Ephesus Paul would write, "Finally, be strong in the Lord and in his mighty power."[2] The Apostle himself had experienced the Lord's empowerment in the midst of his own human weakness when he heard Him say, "My grace is sufficient for you, for my power is made perfect in weakness."[3] God's mighty power is more than a match for our human weakness.

A little old woman once lived in a valley tucked away in the mountains. They lit their home with kerosene lamps. She decided that they really ought to have the availability of electric power, so she campaigned to get the electric company to come all the way out to their little house and install it. Subsequently the electric company installed, and then monitored, the usage of electricity. They discovered that it amounted to almost nothing at all.

They sent a service rep to see her. "After all the trouble you took to petition us to install electricity in your house, don't you even bother to use it?" "Oh sure," she answered." We turn it on every night when it gets dark, so we will be able to see enough to light our kerosene lamps." That's sort of how we Christians implement the power of God.[4] All that infinite power is available to us, but we resort to it only in emergencies. We tend to use God's power, not as a first resort but as a last resort.

"...strengthened with all power according to his glorious might so that you may have great endurance and patience..."[5] A small, fearless band of determined Christians were accustomed to meeting at a secret location, evading the watchful eyes of the Atheistic State. They were finally betrayed by an informant who showed the secret police where to find them. With a contingent of armed men, the police took all of them by surprise, interrupting their prayer meeting.

Contemptuously, the captain carefully studied the faces of his captives. He then ordered one of his men to collect the names of each one present at this Christian meeting. Thirty men and women! Just then, an old man stepped forward to contest the count. "You said thirty, but there are thirty one." The officer answered, "We've counted each one of you, and there are exactly thirty." The old man replied, "But there's one you overlooked. He is the Lord Jesus Christ."[6] And Jesus said, "For where two or three come together in my name, there am I with them."[7]

As a young University student, John Wesley - the future founder of Methodism - was somewhat arrogant and self-centered. He possessed a brilliant intellect and certain social advantages. Then, one night, he had a change of attitude. He happened to be conversing with a homeless person. He also happened to notice that this man displayed an unexplainable sense of contentment. He was even thankful to God. Wesley was mystified. He asked this impoverished man, with barely suppressed sarcasm, "What do you have to be grateful about?" The poor man responded, "I thank the Lord for giving me my life, a heart to love Him, and a constant desire to serve Him." John Wesley was deeply touched and chastened. He saw that this man knew the richness of a vital relationship with God.[8]

"...joyfully giving thanks to the Father..."[9]

In fact, giving thanks to God changes our attitude. We are given an attitude adjustment, or maybe an attitude transplant. Serendipitously, we discover within ourselves a deep and abiding joy. Once a little boy remarked that "Salt is what ruins mashed potatoes when it's left out." Utilizing that same logic, "Gratitude is what ruins your life when it's left out."[10] So joyfully give thanks to the Father "who has qualified you to share in the inheritance of the saints in the kingdom of light."[11]

In the Roman army, a retiring veteran would receive a piece of land as an "inheritance" for his dedicated service to the Roman Empire. In the same way, each and every Christian, upon retirement from active duty here on earth, will receive an inheritance.[12] Remember what our Lord said on the night that came to be called "The Last Supper": "I am going there to prepare a place for you. And if I go and prepare a place for you, I will come back and take you with me that you also may be where I am."[13]. It's often been said that the Christian life is difficult, but the retirement benefits are out of this world.

A certain man decided that he'd like to travel by ship to see his Swedish relatives. He squirreled away all his money so that he'd be able to purchase a ticket for the cruise line. The ship had a glittering dining room where it offered epicurean meals. Sadly, he knew that he couldn't possibly afford them. So he hoarded crackers and cheese and other snacks. Each night he'd walked on deck and inhale the appetizing aromas of the fabulous dinners. And each night he'd stoically return to his cabin to nibble on cheese and crackers.

Then, the very last evening, he decided to splurge by purchasing one of those tantalizing dinners. As he finished, he tried to pay for his meal. He was shocked to discover that all of those culinary masterpieces were free. They had been included in the price of the ticket.[14] We followers of Jesus often forget about our inheritance. He has prepared everything for us. And it's free. "No eye has seen, no ear has heard, no mind has perceived what God has prepared for those who love him."[15]

Chapter 8: "The Kingdom of the Son" (Col. 1:13 NIV)

Most of my childhood and adolescent years were spent in a little Methodist church in Northeast Philadelphia. Our theology was a little loose and liberal. Nevertheless, we were a warm and loving fellowship of caring Christians. In contrast, my cousins grew up in a Fundamental church whose doctrines were more rigid. They had a long laundry list of infractions that were considered sins: drinking alcoholic beverages, smoking, attending theaters, dancing - the list went on and on. I personally never paid much attention to that list because the "sins" seemed so picayune.

But by the time I reached my early twenties, I began to feel trapped in a suffocating darkness within my own soul. I knew for a fact that I was indeed a "sinner". It wasn't the little missteps that made me a sinner; it was something far more insidious: my incorrigible and relentless self-centeredness that permeated and contaminated everything. As has often been remarked: "We aren't sinners because we sin; we sin because we're sinners." In my heart I knew I needed to be rescued, delivered, set free, "saved". If there really is Savior, I needed to get to know Him.

Paul wrote this: "For he has rescued us from the dominion of darkness and brought us into the kingdom of the Son he loves..."[1] I once heard a Bible scholar say that the whole Bible, from start to finish, is a "Divine rescue story". And the day would come when through prayer, the Divine Rescuer would find me. One poet summarized my experience of personal deliverance when he would write, "Praise, my soul, the King of heaven /to his feet they tribute bring; /Ransomed, healed, restored, forgiven, /Evermore his praises sing."[2]

Paul wrote a colorful word picture: "For he has rescued us from the dominion of darkness..."[3] William Barclay, in his book The Mind of St. Paul, stated that each of us is enchained by the chains we ourselves have fashioned. We are enslaved by weaknesses we ourselves cannot overcome. We find ourselves in bondage to those deeper drives and impulses from which we cannot free ourselves, try as we may. And then Jesus comes and sets us free.[4]

In his book, Our Sufficiency in Christ, John MacArthur recounted the following episode. One day a stranger walked into his office, announcing that he needed help. He was embarrassed to impose upon the pastor's time since, not only wasn't he a parishioner, he wasn't ever a Christian. In fact, he was Jewish. The pastor willingly listened to him as he poured out a difficult problem and described the quagmire in which he was entrapped. First, he had been twice married and divorced. Secondly, he was presently living with another woman just for convenience. Thirdly, he was a medical doctor whose specialty was performing abortions. Now he felt utterly lost. He turned to the pastor and asked, hesitantly, "Can you help me?" "No," answered the pastor, pausing to create a greater impact, "But I know Someone who can."[5]

The pastor then began to tell the distraught physician about Jesus. The doctor interrupted him. "Look, you're talking about this Jesus, and I don't even know who he is." "Would you like to get to know Him?" "Sure." "Here's a Bible. Read through John. Just keep reading until you know who He is. And then come back and see me."

A few days later John MacArthur was relating this incident to a fellow pastor who then proceeded to challenge him. "Is that all you said to him? Just 'Read John?' Didn't you offer him any books or tapes?" John MacArthur assured his puzzled friend that this is all that he felt required to do because the Gospel, all by itself, is powerful. If anyone has an open heart, the Holy Spirit can do the rest.

Less than one week later he received a phone call from the doctor, wanting to arrange an appointment. "Now I know who He is. I've made the decision to receive Him into my heart as soon as I can clean up my act." "No, that's not the way to go. Instead, ask Jesus into your heart and then let Him clean up your act." That is just what the doctor did. And that is just what Jesus did.[6] So Paul wrote, "For he has rescued us from the dominion of darkness and brought us into the kingdom of the Son he loves..."[7]

A ragged boy in filthy clothes stepped into the interior of a London orphanage. He came there looking to be sheltered because he felt afraid and vulnerable in the world outside. The director of the home was there in the lobby. He stopped him and asked, "What are you doing here?" The little boy replied, "I'd really like to live here." "Yes, but who are you? Listen, we don't even know who you are." The boy stood there, bewildered.

"Do you have any references?" The young boy stood there, trying hard to process that question. The director tried again, "Do you have any recommenders?" The boy took off his torn, dirty coat and extended it to the director. "Please, sir, I figured that this is all I would need." In one wonderful moment, the orphanage director swept the little boy up in his arms and took him in, where he would be fed, clothed, warmed, accepted, and loved. That's a picture of our meeting with Jesus.[8]

When we come to Him, we might have nothing or no one to recommend us. Yet, He's here and He cares. The prophet Isaiah wrote, "All of us have become like one who is unclean, and all our righteous acts are like filthy rags..."[9] But Jesus makes all the difference. When we come to Him, everything changes. In 1 Peter we read: "But you are a chosen people, a royal priesthood, a holy nation, a people belonging to God, that you may declare the praises of him who called you out of darkness into his wonderful light."[10]

Chapter 9: "Redemption" (Col. 1:14 NIV)

Paul was reminding the Colossians of everything that the Lord had done for them. He might do the same with you. He says, "Remember!" Remember how your life was before you met Jesus. Remember your darkness, your lostness, your disorientation. Remember! "For he has rescued us from the dominion of darkness and brought us into the kingdom of the Son he loves, in whom we have redemption, the forgiveness of sins."[1]

Redemption! That means to redeem, to buy back, to reclaim. Let's say that you take a personal possession, something of perhaps material or sentimental value, to the pawn shop and leave it there on the shelf. Then, sometime later, when the circumstances allow, you decide to reclaim it, to redeem it, to buy it back. And it's yours once more[2]. To the Christians in the church at Corinth Paul wrote, "You are not your own; you were bought at a price."[3]

What does that mean? You had sold yourself to "the world, the flesh, and the Devil." You wound up enslaved and could not free yourself. But Jesus paid the price to buy you back. Therefore you no longer belong to yourself or anyone else or anything else; you belong to Him. And what was the price He paid for you? "For you know that it was not with perishable things such as silver or gold that you were redeemed..., but with the precious blood of Christ..."[4]

At a time in American history when the slave trade was still legal, a certain gentleman inadvertently walked into a slave auction. A platform had been erected on the main street. It had attracted a large and curious crowd. He stood there, mesmerized, as one slave after another was paraded before the audience. Half-naked, in shackles, each was presented for the bidding. One by one they were auctioned off, like animals. There were those in the crowd who wanted to perform their personal inspection by rubbing their hands over the slave.

Up to now this gentleman was just another onlooker. Now he began to look intently at the group of slaves still waiting to make their debut on the platform. He noticed a frightened girl in the back of the group, crouching as if hiding herself from this indignity. She was trembling with fear. Suddenly, amidst the spirited bidding, this gentleman shouted out a bid that was double the amounts being offered. In fact, it proved to be double any amount being offered for any slave that day.

Stunned silence! People could not believe the enormity of the bid. The auctioneer hit the gavel and said, "Sold to the gentleman over there." He made his way through the crowd to the platform and waited for his purchase to be led down the steps to her purchaser. The slave trader took hold of the rope that had restrained his prisoner and placed it in the hand of the stranger who had just bought her. Hastily, she lifted her eyes, looked hard at him, then spit in his face.

He walked her to an open area where all business transactions were completed. Whenever a slave was granted freedom, there was another procedure to be followed. A special legal document, known as "manumission papers," was signed. This stranger signed both. In other words, he paid for her and then officially set her free. She stared at him, confused by what he had just done and what it could possibly mean. He spoke to her, "Do you understand what I've done? Take this document. It shows that you are free and that no one can ever make you a slave again."

She spoke hesitantly, "Are you telling me that you set me free? Is that what you're saying?" He nodded. She slipped down on her knees and wept at his feet, overcome with emotion. Then she stammered, "You set me free; I will serve you forever." Once each of us was bound up by sin. Jesus came into our life and freed us from our bondage. And that's what scripture calls "Redemption."[5] The Lord says, "I have swept away your offenses like a cloud, your sins like the morning mist. Return to me, for I have redeemed you."[6]

But think about this. How could a man's sacrifice 2,000 years ago and 6,000 miles away possibly have anything to do with us, with me, with you? Calvary was literally "long ago and far away"! Furthermore, this earthly Jesus, this Galilean Jew, did not know you and me, did not know our parents or grandparents or great grandparents, either. The two events - his death and our sin - are far removed in space and time.

In order to shed more light on this conundrum, I first need to share with you a scientific consensus: The speed of light is the fastest force in the universe, precisely 186,272 miles per second. So nothing generally is traveling faster than that.[7] Tony Campolo, in his book How to be Pentecostal Without Speaking in Tongues, wrote the following fascinating explanation:

According to Albert Einstein's Theory of Relativity, if - hypothetically - we were to set you in a rocket ship and propel you into space at 170,000 miles per second (which is quite a bit fast, but still slower than the speed of light) and instructed you to return in 10 years, something rather strange would occur. Returning in 10 years, relative to your time, you'd be startled to learn that all the rest of us earthlings would actually be twenty years older. In other words, according to Einstein, our 20 years on earth would pass by in just 10 years of your time. (How's that for "holding your age"?)

If you, in your rocket ship, were to close in on the speed of light - let's say, reaching the speed of 180,000 miles per second - the results would be even stranger. When one day went by, relative to your time, all of us here on earth would wind up being 20 years older. And if you really "put the pedal to the metal," and actually traveled the speed of light (186,272 miles per second) you'd experience all human time at once. (I don't think that Dr. Albert Einstein or Dr. Tony Campolo expected this to make sense to the reader, but presumably that's the way it is.) All of human time would be contemporaneous for you. Everything would be right now.

Then, in conclusion, Tony added this very big thought. He said that the reason he took the reader on this journey into relativity and quantum physics was to set you up to understand how you, and the cross of 2,000 years ago, can be together right now in God's sight.[8] So, you see, Jesus' death on the cross is not "ancient history". It's not something that happened "long ago and far away". It's right now. The cross is standing right here, right now, and you are standing beneath it. How should you respond? The same way as that slave girl who stammered, "You set me free; I will serve You forever."

Chapter 10: "He is the Image of the Invisible God" (Col. 1:15a NIV)

Writing about Jesus, Paul brazenly declared, "He is the image of the invisible God..."[1] Michael Green, professor of Evangelism and New Testament at Vancouver's Regent College, wrote the following thought about "the invisible God". He asked us to recall that, when the first Russian cosmonaut returned to earth, he cavalierly proclaimed that God doesn't exist because he had not managed to bump into Him in outer space. That's like saying that a certain artist doesn't exist because you didn't happen to see him on his painting, forgetting that there wouldn't even be a canvas to exhibit if the artist had not shown himself in every brush stroke.[2]

The dumbest assumption is that if you don't see Him, He simply doesn't exist. Leslie Weatherhead wrote about a fascinating parable he had read in The Observer (April 7, 1963), in which the reader was to imagine a family of mice who lived in a concert piano. That large piano was their whole world, their entire universe. Every now and then, beautiful music floated over them, enveloped them, inspired them. They were always impressed by the miraculous music. It gave them great peace to know that, even though the music maker was unseen, his music was close to them. It gave the mice great pleasure to believe in the Unseen Player who made music in their lives.

Then one day a particularly adventurous and daring mouse decided to explore his world - the hidden, dark spaces. So he climbed up into the inner-workings of the piano. He returned, very pensive. He had discovered how the music was actually produced. The whole secret was little wires, stretched taut. They vibrated. And that's what made the music. Now it was obvious that all the mice would now be obliged to revise their entire belief system. Only the most stalwart believers would continue to believe the myth of the Unseen Player.

Later, another explorer studied the piano's complex mechanism. He refined the theory. The reason that the piano wires vibrated was because they were struck by hammers. These hammers danced across the trembling wires and produced the music. The theory certainly had grown more complicated, but it managed to convince the little mice that they inhabited a purely mechanical, mathematical world. There actually was no Unseen Player. What was invisible simply didn't exist. Every mouse could now understand that this was only a myth. Still, each day, the beautiful music of the Unseen Player continued to float all around them.[3]

"...the invisible God..."[4] We're not entirely comfortable with a God who is invisible. One day, a little boy, walking along with his mother, looked up at the sky and asked her, "Is that where God is?" She replied in the affirmative. He thought about it for a few moments, then said, "Wouldn't it be nice if He'd just stick His head out through the clouds and let us see Him?"[5] That would be great!

Art Linkletter once observed a little boy feverishly drawing some sort of picture. "What are you coloring?" The little guy answered, "I'm making a picture of God." Art Linkletter said to him, "Well, nobody really knows what God looks like!" The little boy answered, "They will now."[6] People want to see the face of God. In his book Basic Christianity, John W. Stott said that when God decided to make Himself known to us, He had to do it in a way we humans could see, hear, and understand. So He clothed Himself in human flesh.[7]

In his majestic prologue, the gospel writer St. John expressed the mystery of the Incarnation in these words: "In the beginning was the Word, and the Word was with God, and the Word was God. He was with God in the beginning. Through him all things were made.[8] ...The Word became flesh and made his dwelling among us. We have seen his glory, the glory of the One and Only, who came from the father, full of grace and truth...No one has ever seen God, but the one and only Son, who is Himself God and is in closest relationship with the Father, has made him known."[9]

Alister McGrath said that we wonder how we can know God, and we wonder what He is like. The Christian answer is that we can know Him best when we look at Jesus, because He's the one who reveals God to us. That's not to say that God cannot be known in other ways; it's just to say that Jesus is the best way, the fullest way, the closest encounter with God we can have.[10] So if you want to know what God is like, don't bother inquiring of cosmonauts or astronauts or little boys with crayons. Look at Jesus. Paul wrote,

"For God, who said, 'Let light shine out of darkness,' made his light shine in our hearts to give us the light of the knowledge of the glory of God in the face of Christ."[11]

In that vision we catch a glimpse of a loving Father who has reached down His hand to save us all.

Chapter 11: "For by Him All Things were Created" (Col. 1:16 NIV)

I think I have deciphered the central message of Colossians in the simple phrase, "All you ever need is Jesus." The heresy that was contaminating the faith of new Christians claimed that one needed Jesus plus something else.[1] You needed Jesus plus secret esoteric knowledge or Jesus plus asceticism or Jesus plus mysticism. But Paul was clearly and emphatically stating that this Jesus is an all-sufficient Savior. Therefore the followers of Christ must turn their backs on all forms of religious syncretism.

The writer of Hebrews began his sermon with these words: "In the past God spoke to our fore-fathers through the prophets at many times and in various ways, but in these last days he has spoken to us by his Son, whom he appointed heir of all things, and through whom he made the universe. The Son is the radiance of God's glory and the exact representation of his being..."[2] Billy Graham once remarked that not only is Jesus like God, but God is like Jesus.[3]

The Apostle Paul wrote, "He is the image of the invisible God... For by him all things were created...He is before all things, and in him all things hold together."[4] Paul piled phrase upon phrase of superlatives in his description of Christ. In the Gospel according to John, there's an intriguing conversation between Jesus and his adversaries. They challenged him, saying, "'Are you greater than our father Abraham? He died, and so did the prophets. Who do you think you are?'

Jesus replied, 'Your father Abraham rejoiced at the thought of seeing my day...' 'You are not yet fifty years old...and you have seen Abraham!' 'I tell you the truth; Jesus answered, 'before Abraham was born, I am.'"[5] The Eternal Christ!

In his profound study. Disappointment with God. Philip Yancey focused his attention on the scripture passage above and offered a picturesque explanation of the eternity of Christ. He said that many people, throughout the years, have wondered what God was doing before His creation. The theologian St. Augustine considered this a ludicrous question because time did not exist before God created it. Augustine had to admit that we humans are time-bound creatures who view everything from the perspective of human time. We have a difficult time contemplating realties outside our experience. Before God created "time" there was only Eternity, and Eternity is always now.

Since Einstein, we have figured out that time is always relative. Here, said Yancey, is an example: On the night of February 23, 1987, an astronomer in Chile happened to observe a gigantic explosion in outer space, a blast so enormous that he could see it plainly without the aid of a telescope. It was the explosion of a supernova which created, in one second, all the energy that our sun releases in 10 billion years. Now here is the mind-boggling question: did this awesome event, occurring February 23, 1987, really occur on that date? Actually, that star exploded 170,00 years ago, but it took the light all that time to reach us.

Then Yancey ventured further. To paraphrase, he said that we should try to imagine God, larger than the entire universe He created. He could simultaneously observe the explosion of the supernova 170,000 years ago and also February 23, 1987. In other words, God saw this moment from the perspective of the original explosion, and what it took another 170,000 years for us to witness. So He is seeing past, present. and future at once.[6]

I quoted Yancey's illustration in order enlarge your imagination so that we might see how great is our God. He is the creator of space and time. He is beyond space and time. He is the God of Eternity. And inasmuch as Jesus Himself, in a way that shall always remain a mystery, participates in the Godhead, then He is likewise Eternal. That's why the Apostle Paul wrote, "He is before all things, and in him all things hold together."[7]

In the course of my pastoral ministry, I've often met individuals whose personality holds the whole family together. All the siblings, cousins, nephews and nieces seem to spontaneously gravitate to this person. When that magnetic person passes from the scene, there is often chaos and dissolution. The entire family frequently disintegrates because it was that person who held it all together. So, in a larger sense, it is Jesus who holds the whole creation together.

Somewhere, many decades ago, I read this vivid illustration. I don't recall who wrote it or in which book I discovered it, but I share it with you. There once was a tiny particle of dust that felt very insignificant. It floated around interstellar space, wondering what the point of it all was. Then, one day, it discovered that there was a Law of Gravity, built into creation itself, that enabled all the planets to hang suspended in space. It was this law that created order. The little piece of dust imagined that the God behind gravity really cared about suns and moons and planets and stars, but certainly not about him: just a microscopic particle of dust! Yet, he continued to float through space, supported and sustained by the same benevolent Hand.

It is written in scripture: "He heals the broken hearted and binds up their wounds. He determines the number of the stars and calls them each by name."[8] Now think of that! The same God who cares about the planets and calls the stars by name is the God who will heal broken hearts. How great is our God! There's an insightful verse which states, "Though the Lord is on high, he looks upon the lowly..."[9] That has been wonderfully paraphrased: "He sits high and looks low." Thanks be to God.

Chapter 12: "Supremacy" (Co. 1:18c NIV)

A wise old Christian once offered some advice to a young minister. He said, "Brother, don't ever try to be a 'big' preacher. Instead, preach a big Savior"[1] One day my former associate pastor and I were debating a basic difference in our philosophies. Our little discussion wasn't just academic; it was practical, because it crucially affected the way each of us saw ourselves, our church, and our ministry. I finally looked hard at my colleague and said, "Listen, Dave. You have to remember that this church we serve isn't your church or my church. It's the congregation's church!"

Dave thought about that for a moment, then said, "No, Jerry. You have to remember that this isn't your church and it isn't my church and it isn't even the congregation's church. It's Jesus' church! He needs to be Lord not only of the church at large, but also of this church." I sat there silently, chastened. He was right. So Paul wrote, "And he is the head of the body, the church; he is the beginning and the firstborn from among the dead, so that in everything he might have the supremacy."[2]

We followers of Jesus can have direct access to Him. William Barclay told a story about a certain Native American who visited a church and wished to join it. The pastor reviewed his request and, recognizing the blatant fact that this man had never before been a member of any church, carefully questioned him. "Why do you want to be a member of a church?" He answered, "One day I happened to read the Gospel of Luke. It painted the picture of a wonderful Savior. I realized that I could have a personal relationship with Jesus without joining any church. But then I went on and read the Book of Acts. Jesus was back in Heaven, sending out His followers to carry on His work. That's what the Church did. I thought about it, and now I want to belong to that church that carries on Jesus' work."[3]

Dr. F.B. Meyer, pastor and evangelist, reached a critical time in his ministry. He felt downcast. Sitting all alone in his study, he said to himself, "My whole ministry is devoid of any power. I'm not bearing any fruit for the Lord." In a moment, Jesus stood right beside him. This celestial figure spoke to him, saying, "Give me all the keys in your life." The vision was so intensely real that the pastor quickly stood up, frisked his own pockets, and pulled from them a bunch of keys. "Here, Lord. Here's all the keys in my life. They're yours."

"Are you sure that you've given me all the keys?" "Well," Meyer stammered, "All except one. It's a key that opens the door to one little room." The ethereal figure standing before him said, "Then I cannot accept the rest of you keys. If you cannot trust me to manage all the rooms in your life, then I will not accept any of the keys you are trying to offer me." Dr. Meyer was heartsick by the thought that Jesus was now distancing Himself from him. He called after Him, "Please don't leave. Come back, and I'll give you all the keys to all the rooms of my life."[4] He has to have supremacy over your life. That's what it means to call Jesus "Lord".

In a large concert hall, the spell-binding 9th Symphony of Beethoven was performed before a wildly enthusiastic audience who gave the orchestra and its conductor, Arturo Toscanini, thunderous applause. During that extended ovation, Toscanini turned back to his musicians and said, "We are nothing; Beethoven is everything!" This is how the orchestra conductor expressed his humble reverence for the composer of the music. In the same way, you and I must give the Lord first place in every area of our life so that we can humbly say, "I am nothing. Jesus is everything."[5]

So much of the time in my ministry I have put Jesus second and myself, first. Many of the worship services, I say with deep shame, have been all about JERRY CROSSLEY preaching about Jesus. He has not had all the keys to all the rooms of my house, and he has not had all of me. The resulting anarchy in my little world promotes chaos instead of peace. Everything is off-center, and I lose my sense of direction and purpose. If your heart is all full of yourself, you don't have much room left for the Lord.

Charles Lamb, a renowned author and essayist, was himself a deeply committed Christian. One evening he was involved in a discussion with a number of intellectual elites who were reflecting on all the illustrious, famous persons, past and present, that they would like to meet. Someone asked, "What if the poet Milton were to walk into the room?" "We'd go wild with applause," they answered. "And suppose William Shakespeare were to appear among us?" Charles Lamb answered pensively, "If William Shakespeare entered this room, I'm sure we'd all rise respectfully to our feet. But if Jesus were to come into this room, we'd each fall down reverently on our knees."[6]

To those Christians in Philippi, Paul quoted the words of an early Christian hymn. At its conclusion came these passionate words, "Therefore God exalted him to the highest place and gave him the name that is above every name, that at the name of Jesus every knee should bow, in heaven and on earth and under the earth and every tongue confess that Jesus Christ is Lord, to the glory of God the Father." Amen.

Chapter 13: "All His Fullness" (Col. 1:19 NIV)

The revered British pulpiteer of the nineteenth century, Charles Haddon Spurgeon, once remarked that he had listened closely to the sermons of many pastors who not once made a reference to Jesus. They somehow managed to deliver their whole message without ever mentioning Him. Suppose, he said, that a baker decided to take a loaf of bread without resorting to its principle ingredient: flour. What would happen? For one thing, he'd probably - and justifiably - be terminated. That same principle should apply to the preacher who omits the main ingredient of the Christian faith. Perhaps his congregation is comprised of people who don't much care about their spiritual life, but those who do should not be treated to a "Christless gospel".[1]

When I was a seminary student, I was privileged to hear a young preacher offer his analogy. He said that many people, imagining themselves to be a Christian, have never actually received Him into their heart as their personal Lord and Savior. If one takes the word CHRISTIAN and just removes the first syllable, CHRIST, one is left with only three letters: IAN. Many who call themselves CHRISTIAN are really only IANs. Jesus once said, "I am the vine; you are the branches. If a man remains in me and I in him, he will bear much fruit; apart from me you can do nothing."[2] See? Without CHRIST, IAN. Without CHRIST, "I Am Nothing." And that's what IAN stands for!

Paul wrote, "For God was pleased to have all his fullness dwell in [Jesus]..."[3] How could all of God's fullness dwell in a man, a mere mortal? That's a perplexing question that has taxed and tormented theologians and philosophers down through the ages. Our whole faith, it seems to me, centers on a trinity of mysteries. First, the Incarnation (How does God become man?). Second the Atonement (How does one man's death make us "at-one" with God?) And, thirdly, the Resurrection (How can one man's survival of death insure our own?).

There's a lovely hymn that describes each of those three mysteries:

"I know not how that Bethlehem's babe
Could in the God-head be;
I only know the manger child
Has brought God's life to me.

"I know not how that Calvary's cross
A world from sin could free.
I only know its matchless love
Has brought God's love to one.

"I know not how that Joseph's tomb
Could solve death's mystery.
I only know a living Christ,
Our immortality."[4]

So when we reflect on all the fullness of God indwelling Jesus, I think of the words of the hymn, "I only know the manger child has brought God's life to me." John, in the prologue to his gospel, wrote, "In the beginning was the Word, and the Word was with God, and the Word was God. He was with God in the beginning...The Word became flesh and made his dwelling among us."[5]

Someone once showed a man a glass bottle, colored ruby red. "What do you think is in this?" he asked. "Do you think it's some kind of wine? Something the color of burgundy?" The other man could not even hazard a guess. "The answer is milk!" Milk? The ruby red bottle disguised it. He just did not believe it until he saw the milk being poured out into a glass. So it is that Jesus' common, ordinary human container effectively concealed the divinity he contained. Others could see our Lord's humanity but tended to miss His divinity.[6]

During what came to be called "The Last Supper", on the very night before His crucifixion, Jesus engaged in a critical conversation with His followers: "'I am the way and the truth and the life. No one comes to the Father except through me. If you really knew me, you would know my Father as well. From now on, you know him and have seen him.' Philip said, 'Lord, show us the Father and that will be enough for us.' Jesus answered: 'Don't you know me, Philip, even after I have been among you such a long time? Anyone who has seen me has seen the Father...'"[7]

From a fascinating book entitled A Scientific Approach to Biblical Mysteries comes the following illustration: You're standing on a beach looking as far out as you can see. The huge ocean occupies your whole vision. It's all sea, as far as you can see. There are different aspects of this sea. Sometimes it's turbulent and tempestuous; other times, smooth as glass. You watch it intently and observe a cresting wave, far out, gathering speed and intensity as it nears shore. It's still part of the sea, but, in a way, it has a life of its own.

It collides with the beach, then withdraws back into the ocean. Even though, for a moment, the cresting wave seemed to have its own identity, there never was a time when it was not part of the sea. So Jesus came from God and returned to God, Yet there never was a moment when he was not part of him. Just as the wave demonstrates the character of the ocean, even so Jesus demonstrates the character of God. If you've seen a wave, then you have seen the ocean. If you've seen Jesus, then you have seen God.[8]

Chapter 14: "Peace Through His Blood" (Col. 1:20b NIV)

It happened when a large revival was taking place at the Golden Gate Exposition in San Francisco. As the preacher spoke, a growing number of people were becoming aware that he was not entirely in the mainstream of an Evangelical faith. He was certainly an eloquent speaker, but apparently he did not espouse the Biblical understanding of Jesus' substitutionary sacrifice on the cross. He belittled the thought that Jesus died for each of us, that He took our place somehow.

When he at last finished his long diatribe against Jesus' vicarious death, a little old lady in the audience rose to her feet and began to sing William Cowper's inspired and inspiring hymn, "There is a Fountain Filled with Blood". It demonstrated her own rebuttal to the ridicule of the preacher. The words and music drifted across the crowd like a breath of fresh air: "And sinners plunged beneath that flood /Lose all their guilty stains."[1]

The crowd sat in hushed silence. Gradually, scores of people, then, hundreds rose to their feet and began to join in that hymn. By the third verse, probably over a thousand Christian men and women were standing, as a proclamation of their faith, and singing these captivating words, "Dear dying Lamb, thy precious blood /Shall never lose its power, /Till all the ransomed church of God /Be saved, to sin no more."[2] Many of the people who attended the revival were deeply moved - not by the guest preacher but by one courageous old lady who had fearlessly declared her faith.[3]

At the foot of that cross is where our faith begins. Many times I have heard, "You cannot understand the cross until you first stand under the cross." In one of the most impassioned passages in all of scripture, St. Paul wrote, "You see, at just the right time, when we were still powerless, Christ died for the ungodly. Very rarely will anyone die for a righteous man, though for a good man someone might possibly dare to die. But God demonstrates his own love for us in this: While we were still sinners, Christ died for us."[4]

To the Colossians Paul wrote, "For God was pleased to have all his fullness dwell in [Jesus], and through him to reconcile to himself all things, whether things on earth or things in heaven..."[5] Again, in Corinthians he wrote, "that God was reconciling the world to himself in Christ, not counting men's sins against them."[6]

The word "reconciliation" sounds so abstract, but my best illustration comes from my own personal experience. When I was a teenager, I tended to be the center of a group of young men who gravitated around me. (On second thought, the real attraction might not have been I, but my house. They always hung around at my house, draped over every piece of furniture we had.) Then came "the new guy on the block": Stosh. He was a natural charmer, an all-round athlete (An All American in two sports at the same time: soccer and baseball). Now the spotlight subtly shifted from me to Stosh.

I found myself growing jealous. So I looked for, and found, an opportunity to cut him down to size. I strongly, and wrongly, implied that he had taken advantage of all of them in our "crowd". Of course it wasn't true. But after all, "What is truth?" I was more than willing to sacrifice the truth. When Stosh discovered what I had said behind his back, he was enraged. He came within a hair's breadth of attacking me, but walked away, stating that I wasn't worth that expenditure of pugilistic energy.

In the painful months of estrangement that followed, I was filled with shame and actually began to agree with Stosh; I had diminished myself. I really wasn't worth it! Then, one day, he came to my front door and invited me to his party. "Jer, we're having a New Year's Eve party at my house, and I'd like you to come. It won't be much of a party without you."

I just stood there in a state of shock. I felt many emotions all at once. I felt deep guilt because I had worked overtime to destroy his reputation. I felt shame that he had come to me when I was just too embarrassed to come to him. I felt joy that he had somehow found it possible to forgive me. I felt elation that our friendship was repaired, that we were reconciled, that we could go on. In fact, I never got over what he did that day. I had obviously wronged him. I was the one at fault, yet he came to me. It's a memory I pray that I'll never forget.[7] For that is just what God did for us in Christ Jesus. When we were too guilty and ashamed, and - in a way - too proud to come to Him, He came to us.

So Paul wrote, "...and through him to reconcile to himself all things, whether things on earth or things in heaven, by making peace through his blood, shed on the cross."[8]

E. Stanley Jones related a story about a husband who, we might say, was a lucky man whose wife was beautiful, intelligent, and loving. Yet, whenever he went away on his business trips, he would engage in sexual dalliances. Not aware of her husband's amorous affairs, she loved and trusted him. His sin of betrayal began to tear him apart. He couldn't carry his burden any longer, but was afraid that if he told her the truth, she would leave him. Filled with guilt and self-reproach, he told her about his affairs.

He later said that he would never forget her reaction. Processing what her husband was telling her, and realizing the enormity of his betrayal, she collapsed. The depth of her grief, the expression on her face crumpled in despair, tore him up inside. Then she stood on her feet. He was anticipating a barrage of accusations and acrimony, but none of that was forthcoming. Instead with a voice of quiet calm, she said, "I still love you and stand by you." He could hardly believe it. When he saw and realized what his sin had cost her, he was redeemed. Capable of bearing her husband's sin, she could forgive. In the pain and passion of his wife's love, he stepped up to the cross. For now he suddenly understood that His is what the Lord has done for us. He reaches to you and me with love and forgiveness. And we are redeemed.[9]

Chapter 15: "Without Blemish" (Col. 1:22 NIV)

I remember how I saw the world and my place in it before I came to Jesus. I was what is called "a practical atheist". In other words, I didn't say "There is no God." I said, "There is no God for me." I conceded that there was some sort of Deity that was Lord of the universe, but I happened to be the Lord of my own sweet life. Any of you ever think like that? Remember the poem "Invictus" by William Ernest Henley? Its sophomoric phrases spoke to me and for me. It begins:

"Out of the night that covers me,
Black as the Pit from pole to pole,
I thank whatever gods there be
For my unconquerable soul."

And the poem ends with these brazen words:

"It matters not how strait the gate.
How charged with punishments the scroll,
I am the master of my fate:
I am the captain of my soul."[1]

So Paul wrote, "Once you were alienated from God and were enemies in your minds because of your evil behavior."[2] He got that right. There were many Biblical passages that speak of our estrangement from God. For instance, Isaiah wrote, "Surely the arm of the Lord is not too short to save, nor his ear too dull to hear. But your iniquities have separated you from your God; your sins have hidden his face from you, so that he will not hear."[3] And St. John wrote, "This is the verdict: Light has come into the world, but men loved darkness instead of light because their deeds were evil."[4] We are so lost that we don't know we're lost.

Someone wrote that a yacht was in trouble. It was sinking off the California Coast and radioed an emergency message to the U.S. Coast Guard. The owner of the yacht, a famous businessman, was desperate. "My yacht is sinking." "Sir, we are on our way. What's your position?" The owner proudly responded, "I happen to be Chairman of the Board of First National Trust." But that was only his "position" on land; it wasn't his position at sea. And this yachtsman was certainly adrift. His real position was the he was lost and had to be found. That is our position, too.[5]

He sacrificed Himself for you "to present you holy in his sight, without blemish..."[6] He has chosen to forgive you. We frequently use the little expression, "forgive and forget." But sometimes the infraction is so enormous that we can't forget. It's impossible. Providentially the act of forgiveness is not contingent upon the act of forgetting. We can forgive even though we still painfully remember. Forgiveness just means that we don't spend any time or energy recalling the sin or obsessing over it. Instead we simply ask, "Where do we go from here?" And that's what the Lord asks of us.

"...continue in your faith, established and firm, not moved from the hope held out in the gospel."[7] At the end of his life, and facing the distinct possibility that he would be executed, Paul wrote a personal letter to his young protégé Timothy, in which he stalwartly reaffirmed his faith. It's a memorable passage: "For I am already being poured out like a drink offering, and the time has come for my departure. I have fought the good fight, I have finished the race, I have kept the faith. Now there is in store for me the crown of righteousness, which the Lord, the righteous Judge, will award me on that day..."[8]

A dynamic preacher and intellect of the nineteenth century, Henry Ward Beecher, decided to take a math course in college. It was taught by a professor who, even though he was acknowledged to be a genius, was a notorious eccentric. One morning he entered his classroom, scribbled a mathematical problem on the blackboard, and then challenged his students to solve it. One student rushed up the blackboard and wrote the formula that solved the problem. "Wrong!" said the professor. Confused and uncertain, the young man returned to his seat.

Then Henry Ward Beecher walked forward, picked up the chalk, and proceeded to write the very same solution offered by the first student. The professor said, "I already told you that was wrong. Are you deliberately trying to contradict me?" "No sir, I'm not. But I know in both my head and my heart that this answer is right!" The professor smiled. "Yes, Beecher, you're quite right. The answer is right." The teacher then turned to his startled students and said, "You are going to be tomorrow's leaders. It's not enough to tell others that you have the right answers. You'll have to show them that you believe in your answers."[9]

We have the answer to life's problems: Jesus. You know the answer. Now believe in it.

Chapter 16: "Rejoice in What Was Suffered" (Col. 1:24 NIV)

Jesus had warned His followers that if they really wanted to follow Him, they'd have to be prepared to suffer." Then Jesus said to his disciples, 'If anyone would come after me, he must deny himself and take up his cross and follow me. For whoever wants to save his life will lose it, but whoever loses his life for me will find it."[1] And, to the Colossians, the Apostle Paul wrote, "Now I rejoice in what was suffered for you..."[2] What "sufferings" did Paul himself suffer for the sake of spreading the Gospel?

He enumerated those sufferings in 2 Corinthians: "I have worked much harder, been in prison more frequently, been flogged more severely, and been exposed to death again and again. Five times I received from the Jews the forty lashes minus one. Three times I was beaten with rods, once I was stoned, three times I was shipwrecked, I spent a night and a day on open sea, I have been constantly on the move. I have been in danger from rivers, in danger from bandits, in danger from my own countrymen, in danger from Gentiles; in danger in the city, in danger in the country, in danger at sea; and in danger from false brothers. I have labored and toiled, and have often gone without sleep; I have known hunger and thirst and have often gone without food; I have been cold and naked."[3]

That's quite a list! Paul was so intent on following Jesus that he allowed himself to become a moving target. He even wrote, "Now I rejoice in what was suffered for you..."[4] I know there are people, with a sad psychological aberration, who are always seeking martyrdom. However, we are not advocating seeking suffering for suffering's sake, but enduring suffering for Jesus' sake. Jesus concluded his Beatitudes with this thought: "Blessed are you when people insult you, persecute you and falsely say all kinds of evil against you because of me. Rejoice and be glad, because great is your reward in heaven, for in the same way they persecuted the prophets who were before you."[5]

One day someone caught sight of a soldier who had been grievously wounded in battle. The person who noticed him there, with one leg missing, said, "I'm sorry that you had to lose your leg," to which the soldier responded, "I didn't have to lose my leg; I gave it."[6] Paul wrote these words to the Christians in Philippi: "For it has been granted to you on behalf of Christ not only to believe on him, but also to suffer for him..."[7] After the blinding light on the road to Damascus stopped Saul of Tarsus in his tracks, the Lord came to a Christian named Ananias and commanded him to visit this former persecutor of the Church. Ananias was, understandably, reticent. He was, in other words, dragging his feet. "But the Lord said to Ananias, 'Go! This man is my chosen instrument to carry my name before the Gentiles and their kings and before the people of Israel. I will show him how much he must suffer for my name.'"[8]

A Chinese Christian woman, sickly but saintly, struggled through physical afflictions, emotional disruptions in her life, and a great deal of rejection. For this woman, Christiana Tsai, was a devout follower of Jesus who, for years, had tried in vain to lead her family members to Christ. Through the years they had completely ignored her. Then, one day, one of her brothers gathered together the whole family for an important announcement. They were puzzled by what he was going to tell them, but, at the same time, they were curious. So, complying with his summons, they came together.

He explained to them that, for years, he had persistently rejected his sister's pleadings. Yet, all that time, he had observed the way she confronted her suffering. He concluded that the only way that she could endure all this constant barrage of pain and suffering was the strong probability that she had "invisible means of support". So he picked up her Bible and began to read it. He realized soon enough that he was a sinner and received Jesus as Lord and Savior. That was his announcement, that was the message that he wanted to share with his family.

Later, Christiana expressed her joy and sense of wonder. It amazed her that this same brother who had torn her Bible to shreds and had invented ways to persecute her was the brother who had now accepted Christ.

Furthermore, ever since his forthright confession of faith, other family members had also become Christians.[9] The suffering, pain, and rejection had all been worth it. It is written in 1 Peter 4:12-13 NIV: "Dear friends, do not be surprised at the painful trial you are suffering, as though something strange were happening to you. But rejoice that you participate in the sufferings of Christ, so that you may be overjoyed when his glory is revealed."

Chapter 17: "The Mystery" (Col. 1:26 NIV)

"I have become [the Church's] servant by the commission God gave me to present to you the word of God in its fullness..."[1] God had called him to bring those in darkness into His light. Way back in the Old Testament book of Deuteronomy Isaiah the prophet had written, "Arise, shine, for your light has come, and the glory of the Lord rises upon you. See, darkness covers the earth and thick darkness is over the peoples, but the Lord rises upon you and his glory appears over you. Nations will come to your light, and kings to the brightness of your dawn."[2]

His calling was "to present to you the word of God in its fullness - the mystery that has been kept hidden for ages and generations..."[3] A mystery is something that can be known only through revelation.[4] Presumably, it's something God wants us to know. I think the mystery is that God is here among us, with all of us; no one is left out of His love unless they exclude themselves. Why? "For God so loved the world!"[5]

So Paul spoke about "the mystery that has been kept hidden for ages and generations, but is now disclosed to the saints."[6] Once Jesus had said to His disciples, "There is nothing concealed that will not be disclosed or hidden that will not be made known. What I tell you in the dark, speak in the daylight; what is whispered in your ear, proclaim from the roofs."[7] In the opening chapter of John's Gospel we read about the inclusivity of God's love: "He was in the world, and though the world was made through him, the world did not recognize him. He came to that which was his own, but his own did not receive him. Yet to all who received him, to those who believed in his name, he gave the right to become children of God - children born not of natural descent, nor of human decision or a husband's will, but born of God."[8]

Marilyn Helleberg wrote that she once heard a story about an ancient Greek monastery that, in its day, had been a religious center where a large number of monks resided. It had been like a Christian mecca for the population around it. That was a long time ago. Now its number was gravely diminished. In fact, there were only a handful of monks remaining. One day the Abbot visited an old, familiar friend and poured out to him the story of its sad decline.

His long-time friend listened closely, then said, "I have a secret to share with you." "A secret? Tell me what it is." His friend grew quiet, reflective, and leaned towards him. He bent over near his ear and whispered, "The Messiah is with you. He's already in your monastery, among your number." The Abbot knew that his friend would not joke about this. He knew his revelation must be true.

He quickly returned to his monastery and summoned his monks together. "Listen carefully because I have a secret - a wonderful secret - to share with you. Here it is: the Messiah is right here among us." The monks were shocked. They began to question themselves. "Which one is the Messiah? Could it be Brother Anthony? Or maybe Father Timothy?" Since they never could be sure which one of them was the Messiah in disguise, each monk tried to be kind and generous to all the rest.

Well, soon enough the word got out to everyone that this mysterious monastery was a special place where all the residents loved and served one another. Everybody in that century-old monastery went out of their way to be kind. Soon scores of applicants came, wanting to join and wanting to learn that special secret. Now, said the author, when we sit together in worship, imagine that someone has whispered a secret into your ears: "The Messiah is right here. He is already among you." Perhaps that will make a difference in the way we see and treat each other. "Because, you know, the secret is true."[9]

Chapter 18: "Christ in You, the Hope of Glory" (Col. 1:27 NIV)

Sometimes we are astounded by God's apparent choices. He occasionally chooses those whom we might consider the worst possible candidates. Frequently I've wanted to volunteer to be His personnel manager. Yet He persists in arranging things without me. I guess that's why He's God, and I'm not. For instance, I remember a Prayer & Praise meeting one evening in a church I was pastoring. Our young people were searching our community for "lost souls".

That night they carried into our Fellowship Hall a young man who had passed out on drugs. Keough was part-Cheyenne Native American. He had long black hair, ear bangles, and a drug-induced stupor. They laid him down on the floor, surrounded him, and prayed very vocally for him. I felt annoyed. I knew that their heart was in the right place but inwardly felt that they were misguided. Why had they wasted my time and theirs by bringing such a "basket case" into our church? He didn't know what they were saying or praying. They leaned close to his ear and repeated, "Jesus love you, and we love you too."

He came to Christ! Unbelievable! And he would become a clarion call, a crystal clear voice that would lead others to the Lord. He would become active in mission outreaches. He would be a luminous beacon in others' darkness. He was such an odd choice. However, this is the one that the Lord would use.

To the Colossians, Paul wrote that "God has chosen to make known among the Gentiles the glorious riches of this mystery..."[1] The Gentiles, of all people. The Jewish Christians, in Jerusalem and all Judaea, naturally assumed that, in order to be saved, you must first become a Jew. That almost went without saying. Each male first needed to be circumcised and profess obedience to the Law in its entirety (some 613 Mosaic laws). Yet here was Simon Peter, rising to his feet, to offer another perspective:

"God, who knows the heart, showed that He has accepted [the Gentiles] by giving the Holy Spirit to them, just as he did to us. He made no distinction between us and them, for he purified their hearts by faith...We believe it is through the grace of our Lord Jesus that we are saved, just as they are."[2] A beautiful hymn summarizes the argument when it says, "In Christ there is no East or West, /In Him no South or North, /But one great fellowship of love /Throughout the whole wide earth."[3]

"...God has chosen to make known among the Gentiles the glorious riches of this mystery..."[4] Part of the mystery of God's election is that He loves Gentiles as much as He loves Jews. Remember when Jesus' parents brought their little child to the Temple, to be dedicated. An old man named Simeon was promised by God that he wouldn't die until he had personally seen God's messiah. So I think that he probably hung around the Temple, imagining that a grown, adult Messiah would ultimately come there. Then, one day, he sees a mother carrying her infant son and knows in a moment that this is He!

Mary is shocked when this old man swoops in and scoops up the child from her arms, all the while saying, "Sovereign Lord, as you have promised, you now dismiss your servant in peace. For my eyes have seen your salvation, which you have prepared in the sight of all people, a light for revelation to the Gentiles and for glory to your people Israel."[5] "To the Gentiles"!

"...God has chosen to make known among the Gentiles the glorious riches of this mystery, which is Christ in you..."[6] In his great book, Ring of Truth, J.B. Philipps discussed his own, deep, growing appreciation of the Bible. He said that, as he studied scripture, the world and the language of the New Testament become very real. One of the things he figured out involved that word "mystery". The simple meaning is that Christ comes to live in the heart of His followers. No other religion talks about God living within a person, living in the heart of one who is open to His love.[7] "Christ in you"! That's the reason for our joy. Instead of your trying to live your life for Him, permit Him to live His life through you.[8]

"...Christ in you, the hope of glory."[9] Eugene Peterson, in The Message, writes this beautiful paraphrase: "The mystery in a nutshell is just this: Christ is in you, therefore you can look forward to sharing in God's glory. It's that simple."[10] You, personally, are privileged to entertain that thought. Does that suggest that you can "ride on Jesus' coat tails" to Heaven? You bet!

Chapter 19: "We Proclaim Him" (Col. 1:28a NIV)

Many preachers preach psychology; many, morality; many, ethics; many, philosophy; many, politics. But there's really only one thing that we preachers should focus upon. The Apostle Paul wrote, "We proclaim him..."[1] All that other stuff that becomes the substance of sermons might be fascinating; but it doesn't save anyone. At the very heart of the Gospel is a Person, and we're not really preaching unless we are talking about Him.[2] We aren't saved by theology, by doctrine, by any "ism"; we are saved by a Person. Him we proclaim.

I read this illustration: Years ago two very distinguished scholars were earnestly engaged in conversation. Dr. Howard Lowry, president of Wooster College, was discussing religion with Dr. Radhakrishnan, a Hindu philosopher. Dr. Lowry was reflecting upon his personal embarrassment when he'd listen to other Christians proclaim Jesus as the only Way. In retrospect, he felt that it sounded arrogant to say that. Especially to say that in a country where the Christian population was only ten million out of over four hundred million! It sounded to Dr. Lowry that the Christians were proudly announcing, "We are the only ones with this wisdom." Surprisingly, the Hindu philosopher disagreed. "Don't you see?" he asked. "That is exactly what the Christian must say because that is what their scripture says. If you are a Christian, you cannot say less. As long as what you say is in the spirit of Jesus."[3]

"We proclaim him, admonishing and teaching everyone with all wisdom..."[4] On the African continent, at a mission, a woman became a Christian. Her new-found faith brought her so much joy that she felt she must give something back. However, finding that certain "something" to offer back to the Lord might be difficult because she was old; she was illiterate, and - to top it off - she was blind. She brought her Bible to her missionary teacher and asked him to underline John 3:16. After he complied with her request, she took her Bible and simply seated herself outside the school, with her open Bible on her lap.

At the end of the day, when the students came out of school she would invite them to sit down beside her. Then she would ask them to read the underlined portion. "Do you understand what you are reading?" she'd inquire. And when they answered that they did not, she would take the opportunity to explain it. That's really all she did, and all she knew how to do. Yet, because of her humble service, loving heart, and faithful witness, several young men later entered the ministry: twenty four of them![5]

So we teach with all wisdom - not the wisdom of the world but the wisdom of God. To the Christians in the church at Corinth Paul had written, "Where is the wise man? Where is the scholar? Where is the philosopher of this age? Has not God made foolish the wisdom of the world? For since in the wisdom of God the world through its wisdom did not know him, God was pleased through the foolishness of what was preached to save those who believe. Jews demand miraculous signs and Greeks look for wisdom, but we preach Christ crucified; a stumbling block to Jews and foolishness to Gentiles, but to those whom God has called, both Jews and Greeks, Christ the power of God and the wisdom of God. For the foolishness of God is wiser than man's wisdom, and the weakness of God is stronger than man's strength."[6]

Paul worked hard so that he could present everyone perfect in Christ."[7] Of course we know that "nobody's perfect." We are all aware of that, in others and in ourselves. But I think it means to be perfectly conformed in His image: to look like Him, think like Him, act like Him, respond like Him. So in Romans 8 we find these words inscribed: "For those God foreknew he also predestined to be conformed to the likeness of his son..."[8] That's a big mouthful of words, that, in koine Greek, might have sounded like, "yada yada yada. "What does it mean? God made the Christian to look like Jesus.

There was to be a wedding in a little English village. The family audaciously hired a prestigious pipe organist. He came to the obscure church unsure of what he would find. Just what kind of organ would he be expected to play? When he arrived, it exceeded his worst fears: an old, creaky, wheezy organ. However, he was a consummate musician. As his fingers that day flew over the keys, he made the dilapidated musical instrument actually sound wonderful. God can do the same with you. You might be like that next to worthless musical instrument. Yield yourself to the Lord. As an evangelist once said, let the hands of Christ - hands that stilled the storm, hands that broke the bread and offered the cup, hands that were nailed to a cross - pass over you, touching the keys of your life, and transforming you into an instrument of praise.[9]

Chapter 20: "To This End I Labor" (Col. 1:29 NIV)

The Apostle now reminded his audience that his goal was to "present everyone perfect in Christ. To this end I labor, struggling with all his energy, which so powerfully works in me."[1] Perfect. Mature. All-grown up. Again, his goal is to be like Jesus. If, as a follower of the Lord, we don't look any different, sound any different, think any different, or act any different from anyone else, then no one is going to be interested in the faith we represent. Our refusal to be different will make others indifferent to the One we are championing. We need to reflect Him.

There's a poem I've always loved. Written by Beatrice Clelland (1912-1997), it's simply entitled "Indwelt".

"Not merely in the words you say,
Not only in your deeds confessed,
But in the most unconscious way
Is Christ expressed.

"Is it a beatific smile,
A holy light upon your brown?
Oh no, I felt His Presence while
You laughed just now.

"For me 'twas not the truth you taught,
To you so clear, to me so dim,
But when you came to me you brought
A sense of Him.

"And from your eyes He beckons me,
And from your heart His love is shed,
Till I lose sight of you and see
The Christ instead."

I try, with all my heart (usually) to follow Jesus. I try to be faithful to Him, to live the life He described in the Sermon on the Mount (Matthew 5, 6, 7 - possibly the themes of many of His sermons).I try to be faithful. But I so often fail! I let others down; I let Jesus down. I let myself down. I had a friend, Lee Zengeler, who once said to me, "Look, the Lord doesn't need any more plastic Christians. He's already got millions of them." With the help of the Holy Spirit we are to share with others that Christ is the One they can trust through life, through death, and into Eternity.

And, trusting Him, you can - by an act of your will - entrust yourself to Him. I want to share with you a true story, originally recounted by Oswald J. Smith. Picture this: It's a beautiful golden morning at Niagara Falls, NY. The date is June 30th, 1859. The mighty waterfall thunders onto the rocks 160 feet below. A large crowd has assembled, both above and below the falls. They're filled with excitement because a man, purported to be the greatest tightrope walker in the world, has published in the local newspaper a bold challenge. He, Charles Blondin (real name Jean Francois Gravelet) will walk a tightrope suspended over the falls.

There it is. A tightrope 1,100 feet long has been stretched from riverbank to riverbank. There's no safety net. Delicately balancing himself with a long pole, he ventures forth on the swaying rope, slick with mist, and cautiously begins his slippery walk. Voices in the crowd are hushed into silence. The rope doesn't remain taut; towards the center it sags. That means that the tightrope walker is obliged to walk up towards the opposite shore. This is no "walk in the park".

Then, triumphantly, he plants his foot upon the farther bank, to the thunderous ovation of the crowd, rivaling the roar of the waterfall. He has accomplished a feat that most people would consider to be impossible. Now he turns to the sea of faces surrounding him and proceeds to make a preposterous proposal. He will now attempt to walk back - this time carrying a man on his shoulders. To those within earshot he asks, "Do you think I can do this?" Everyone does. Turning to a possible candidate, he asks, person-to-person, "Do you think I can do it?"

Without hesitation, the onlooker answers," Of course!" "Well, that'll be fine because I'm looking for someone to carry." Immediately his admirer loses his enthusiasm and fades into the crowd. The tightrope walker asks another three, who quickly try to camouflage themselves among other people. They each think that the feat can be accomplished, but they're not going to be the first-class passenger. Finally, he turns to his own manager who has never seen him do this but has faith in him. "I trust you to carry me over the falls."

Breathlessly the crowd watches. He balances his friend and the pole he carries, and then begins his perilous walk. The tightrope walker reaches the center of his course: high above the rushing, broiling water, poised in mid-air. The rope begins swaying wildly. How he manages to maintain his balance no one can understand, for Charles Blondin must instantly make allowances not only for his own shifts in weight but also for those almost imperceptible shifts in the weight of his passenger. At last they reach the other side amidst a wild ovation and an audible exhale from the nervous crowd.

Oswald J. Smith saw a crucial analogy in this picturesque scene. He saw an unforgettable image of our own pilgrimage journey to Heaven. Between these two worlds is one rope that represents salvation. The Lord Himself is the tightrope walker. Think about what transpired that fateful morning. Charles Blondin questioned perhaps five men, who all believed that he could get them across. Only one made it across. Only one actually went. That's because he not only trusted that the tightrope walker could get him there; he trusted enough to entrust himself to him. It's the same with each of us. Trusting is wonderful. Yet it's insufficient. You must trust this Jesus enough to entrust yourself to Him, to place yourself into His hands. He won't lose you.[2]

Chapter 21: "The Mystery of God" (Col. 2:2 NIV)

Sometimes the unexplainable circumstances of our life leave us immobilized. For instance, when we are afflicted with illness, we can quickly feel overwhelmed. We start feeling sorry for ourselves (at least this describes me), and then feel sorry for ourselves feeling sorry for ourselves. Our self-pity can become a bottomless pit. We feel like we are "shut-ins" (shut in by our isolation) and "shut-outs" (shut out of fellowship with others) at the same time.

Yet, in prison, Paul - who had a right to feel cast aside, put on a shelf, locked up and locked out - could still pray. The ceiling of his cell was no barrier to prayer. He wrote to his brothers and sisters in Christ, "I want you to know how much I am struggling for you..."[1] He meant that he was struggling for them in prayer as he brought his petitions before the throne of grace. William Barclay commented that when we are separated from others, the one thing we can do for them is to pray for them.[2]

In James it is written, "The prayer of a righteous [person] is powerful and effective."[3] So many times in my ministry I relied on my own "street smarts" instead of relying on the Lord; I saw prayer as a last resort instead of as a first resort. In prison, Paul could go nowhere, but his prayers could go all the way to Heaven. I visited a member of my congregation who had just survived a critical surgery. There was a chance he would die on the operating table, but a larger chance he'd die without the surgery. It was "touch and go." When I came to see him, he greeted me with a big smile and said, "I felt your prayers."

Paul continued, "My purpose is that [those I am praying for] may be encouraged in heart and united in love..."[4] What was his prayer for all his fledgling believers? That they be encouraged and united in love. If we are not united in love as God's people, then we have ruined our witness. I read that in a certain village in Nigeria there are three hostile, competing churches. One is called "The Church of Christ" and must have been the original fellowship. The second - an obvious break-off - calls itself "The True Church of Christ." And the third has presumptuously awarded itself the title, "The Only True Church of Christ." That's not a very encouraging example of being "united in Love."[5] Remember our Lord's prayer for all of us on the night of the Last Supper? He asked "that all of them may be one, Father, just as you are in me and I am in you. May they also be in us so that the world may believe..."[6]

St. Paul wanted these Christians to experience "the full riches of complete understanding, in order that they may know the mystery of God, namely, Christ, in whom are hidden all the treasures of wisdom and knowledge."[7] In Christ you will find all the deep wisdom and knowledge that you need along your pilgrimage way. You need not go searching for that in eclectic philosophies, in esoteric knowledge. We're not saved by that but only by the Lord in whom knowledge and wisdom meet. All you ever need is Jesus.

Chapter 22: "How Firm Your Faith" (Col. 2:5b NIV)

Whenever I sit down to watch TV, I am almost immediately besieged by a barrage of commercials insisting that I need whatever the sponsors are marketing in order to survive and succeed in life. Well, I think that's what was happening to these hapless Colossians. Every time they turned around, they bumped into someone who was selling them a philosophy or theology or "ism" that they must have. They were just as confused as I can become. Probably, for a limited time, they could get three philosophies for the price of one!

Jesus was all that Christians needed for this life and the life to come. Paul added to his pastoral letter these words, "I tell you this so that no one may deceive you by fine-sounding arguments."[1] In our own idiom, Paul is referring to "smooth words," "slick arguments" by "fast-talkers". He's saying, "Don't let anyone feed you a line."

I remember when I was first a pastor, age 23. Two Jehovah Witnesses knocked on the door of our parsonage in Pocono Lake, PA. Not wanting to be rude, I cautiously invited them into our home. They didn't have reservations, but I certainly did. With a little flourish they presented me with a polished, hardback copy of a textbook published by the Watchtower Society. Then they took out their own copies. "Jerry, would you mind if the three of us read these books together?" They were my guests, and I didn't want to be inhospitable, so I acquiesced.

We all turned to page1. The first Witness would read a paragraph; the second Witness, the following paragraph then I would read the third. So we proceeded. Now, at the bottom of each page, in small print, was a list of questions regarding the text we had all just read. The Jehovah's Witnesses would ask me the questions; I would reply with the "correct" answer; and then they'd make a big fuss over me. I have to admit, their approval felt good.

In other words, suppose the text said, "The purple cow jumped over the moon". One of my guests would direct me to the question at the bottom of the page: "Jerry, what did the cow jump over?" I'd answer, "The moon." The other guest would ask another question at the bottom of the page, "What color was the cow?" And I would dutifully answer, "Purple." At that point they would almost give me a standing ovation, lavishing praise on me. "I believe you're really getting this. You certainly have a sharp mind."

I found myself launching into the next page, and the next, with real enthusiasm. I had new self-confidence, gratitude, and a positive feeling towards my two guests. But gradually I realized that I was being conned by the very process itself. See, I was correctly answering all their questions with all their own answers. They were congratulating me for giving them their answers, which might not have been my own answers. "Just a minute!" I interrupted. "You're congratulating me for giving you your own answers instead of my own." The Witnesses were taken aback. They stood up, excused themselves, and announced, "Then we'll have to shake the dust off our feet and continue on". (A reference to Matthew 10:14.) They had given me insight into the Apostle Paul's admonition, "I tell you this so that no one may deceive you..."[2]

Watch out! All of us can be easily exploited by "fine-sounding arguments".[3] Martin H. Franzmann said that back in the first century A.D., there were some who debated the members of the church using smooth words and arguments that sounded reasonable. After all, they did not dispense with Jesus but merely tried to supplement him.[4] Paul feared that any add-ons would destroy the simple truth of the Gospel.[5]

A young Chinese student was traveling to America, enrolled in one of our universities. He was a deeply committed Christian. Noticing that he was immersed in his Bible, a fellow passenger sauntered over to him and began to hold a conversation. He made an opportunity to run the Bible down, to exhibit his skepticism. Then, after his long diatribe, he added, condescendingly, "I hasten to say that I'm not trying to talk you out of your faith in Christ," to which the student replied, "Sir, if it were possible for you to talk me out of my faith in Christ, He would not be the Savior that He is."[6]

The Apostle was proud of his Colossian Christians who rallied against those who would have perverted that faith. "For though I am absent from you in body, I am present with you in spirit and delight to see how orderly you are and how firm your faith in Christ is".[7] He was using military terms, picturing a disciplined army that formed a solid wall.[8] They stood shoulder to shoulder.[9] Why did he picture them in that way? Because he knew that they'd be going into battle. They would be contending against the forces of darkness for the souls of men and women.

"...how firm your faith in Christ is."[10] It's been said many times, "Keep the faith, and the faith will keep you." An old pastor was reproached one day by one of his parishioners who said, "Pastor, there must be something missing from your ministry. In all of last year, you took only one person into the church - and he's just a young boy." It was true. The minister listened to that accusation with tears in his eyes. "You are right, of course. But I really did try." The only new member was that young boy, Bobby Moffat. The pastor had been faithful. Many years later a world-famous missionary returned from the mission field. Everywhere people spoke his name in reverential tones. For Robert Moffat had won many Africans to the Lord. He once had been a struggling pastor's only convert.[11]

One cold night Robert Moffat, braving the bitter winter, arrived at a church where he was slated to speak and discovered that only a handful of people had showed up. It was a small group of elderly women. He felt very discouraged as he tried to shared his vision of missions with them.

But one small boy trudged through the frigid temperatures that night to pump the bellows of the organ. He was ensconced in the organ loft. He could not help but hear the missionary's challenge. He decided to answer it, go to Africa, and continue to lead men and women to Jesus. That small boy was David Livingstone![12]

Once, in another pastoral letter written to another church, Paul had inscribed these words: "Always give yourself fully to the work of the Lord, because you know that your labor in the Lord is not in vain."[13]

Chapter 23: "Strengthened in the Faith" (Col. 2:7 NIV)

"So then, just as you have received Christ Jesus as Lord, continue to live in him..."[1] One man related his personal struggle to achieve salvation. He endeavored to do more good deeds, read more of the Bible, pray harder, attend more church services - all to no avail. Then someone explained to him that salvation isn't earned; it's free, and all he was required to do was receive it and say, "thank you." He received Christ Jesus and has spent the rest of his life, in word and deed, expressing his gratitude.[2]

"So then, just as you have received Christ Jesus as Lord, continue to live in him..."[3] J.T. Seamands once wrote that we frequently speak about "our living in Christ," and then, "Christ living in us." Which is it? How can we talk about our living in Christ and Christ living in us simultaneously? Do we live in Him? Or does He live in us? A parishioner approached his minister with this conundrum. The pastor picked up a pair of tongs, extended them into his fireplace, and removed a burning ember. "See this ember? The ember was in the fire, but, at the same time, you can see that reddish glow and realize that the fire is in the ember. In exactly the same way, we live our life in Christ while He lives His life in us."[4]

Jesus had said, "I am the vine; you are the branches. If a man remains in me and I in him, he will bear much fruit; apart from me you can do nothing."[5] Hear that? "You in me while I indwell you." It's the ember in the fire while the fire is in the ember. It's part of the incomprehensible mystery of God's self-revelation in Jesus.

"So then, just as you received Christ Jesus as Lord, continue to live in him, rooted and built up in him..."[6] First we have to put down roots. We cannot grow up until we have, first of all, grown down.[7] Chuck Swindoll said something like this: If it's true for trees, it's true for us. Winds of persuasion, bending us irresistibly, storms of controversy beating and battering us, cannot make us budge if our faith is deeply rooted. Like that tree, we will stand immovable. No matter how beautiful the tree's branches, like lattice-work, or how delicately lacy the leaves, only the roots will continue to support us. Passers-by won't notice the roots, but that's what enables the tree to endure.[8] I read that Christians are people who have "invisible means of support."

"So then, just as you received Christ Jesus as Lord, continue to live in him, rooted and built up in him, strengthened in the faith as you were taught, and overflowing with thankfulness."[9] There are terrifying moments in our life that threaten to overwhelm us. In those terrible circumstances, can we still abound in thanksgiving? We gradually come to know, deep within ourselves, that He is still here and with us through it all.

> "When darkness veils his lovely face,
> I rest on his unchanging grace.
> In every high and stormy gale,
> My anchor holds within the veil.
> On Christ the solid rock I stand,
> All other ground is sinking sand."[10]

Chapter 24: "All the Fullness of the Deity" (Col. 2:9 NIV)

Paul had encouraged the Christians of Colossae to live their lives in Jesus.[1] Now he warned them to be on guard against any subtle spiritual seduction.[2] "See to it that no one takes you captive through hollow and deceptive philosophy..."[3] The use of "captive" portrays a kidnapping or an abduction.[4] In other words, don't allow any kind of false teaching parade you around triumphantly. It's easy to be spoofed.

Late one night Mary Baker Eddy, founder of Christian Science, was working overtime, trying to explain her esoteric doctrine to another woman, who remained quite puzzled. "Excuse me, I'm trying hard to follow your thinking. But I still don't understand what you're trying to say. Could you say it more simply?" Mary Baker Eddy responded, "Well, to begin with, you must understand that God is a principle. He's not a 'person'." The woman said, "That's not going to work for me. The God I worship is a Person who revealed Himself in Jesus." And that fundamental truth delivered her from a potentially deceptive philosophy.[5]

In our society we keep generating deceptive slogans: "If it feels good, do it"; "Do your own thing"; "Now is all there is"; "It can't be wrong when it feels so right"; etc. These bits of wisdom set you up for self-destruction. They can be, literally, a death trap. The Rock singer Janis Joplin, less than a year before her death, said, "Sure, I could take better care of myself. I suppose that I could restrict myself to organic food, get a full eight hours of sleep a night, give up smoking and drinking. Maybe it would add a couple of years to my life, but what the hell?!"[6] Duped by the deceptive wisdom of this world, she persisted in "doing her own thing." And she died.

The false teachings that were assaulting these early Christians were strongly suggesting that knowing the Lord wasn't enough to save you. Jesus was not all-sufficient. Jesus was not all you ever need.[7] Instead, to be saved, you needed Jesus plus something else. Today the Jehovah's Witnesses accept the Bible but add the writings of Russell. Christian Science accepts the Bible but then adds the writings of Mary Baker Eddy. The Mormons accept the Bible but then add the Book of Mormon.

Just Jesus! "For in Christ all the fullness of the Deity lives in bodily form..."[8] I believe that Jesus reveals to us the persona, the personality of God. I had a college professor who said, "I believe that one day the disciples looked at this Jesus they were following and said, 'God must be like that.'"[9] On the night of the Last Supper one of Jesus' disciples questioned him. "Philip said, 'Lord, show us the Father and that will be enough for us'. Jesus answered: 'Don't you know me, Philip, even after I have been among you for such a long time? Anyone who has seen me has seen the Father.'"[10]

We come to a marvelous story in the Gospel according to Mark. "A few days later, when Jesus again entered Capernaum, the people heard that he had come home. So many gathered that there was no room left, not even outside the door, and he preached the word to them. Some men came, bringing to him a paralytic, carried by four of them. Since they could not get him to Jesus because of the crowd, they made an opening in the roof above Jesus and, after digging through it, lowered the mat the paralyzed man was lying on."[11]

That reminds me: never let a friend down unless you are letting him down at the feet of Jesus. Jesus must have quickly diagnosed the problem of the man who had just dropped in on Him. What was paralyzing him, what was "tying him up in knots", was his own guilt. If he were ever to walk again, he needed to be forgiven. Jesus therefore said to him, "'Son, your sins are forgiven.' Now some teachers of the law were sitting there, thinking to themselves, 'Why does this fellow talk like that? He's blaspheming! Who can forgive sins but God alone?'"[12]

There's a certain undeniable logic here. Only the one who has been sinned against is entitled to do the forgiving. For instance, if I slam the door on your face, nobody else has the right to forgive me. Only you! If I sin against God, then I must go to Him. So the scribal question hung in the air like a lighted chandelier: "Who can forgive sins but God alone?" "Immediately Jesus knew in his spirit that this was what they were thinking in their hearts, and he said to them, 'Why are you thinking these things? Which is easier to say to the paralytic, "Your sins are forgiven" or to say, "Get up, take your mat, and walk."[13]

Then He added, "'but that you may know that the Son of Man has authority on earth to forgive sins - He said to the paralytic, 'I tell you, get up, take your mat and go home.' He got up, took his mat and walked out in full view of them all. This amazed everyone and they praised God, saying, 'We have never seen anything like this!'"[14]

There is a beautiful poem from the fourth century A.D.:

"Let all mortal flesh keep silence,
And with fear and trembling stand;
Ponder nothing earthly-minded,
For with blessing in his hand,
Christ our God to earth descendeth,
Our full homage to demand."[15]

Chapter 25: "Fullness in Christ" (Col. 2:10 NIV)

Once, when I was attending a dinner meeting, the man seated beside me reached for the pocket inside his suit-coat and mysteriously produced a test tube that was corked. It appeared to contain a murky, greenish fluid. He handed it to me for my further observation of this strange liquid. "What is it?" I inquired. "What do you think it is?" I studied it carefully but could draw no conclusion. So he proceeded to uncork it. "Here, just put a drop on the end of your finger and taste it."

I tasted it, and it burned my tongue. Startled, I asked again, "So, what is it?" Smiling at my obvious discomfiture and confusion, he answered, "It's the Dead Sea!" Wow! The Dead Sea! Of course, it wasn't the whole Dead Sea (difficult to carry in your pocket). Not all the Dead Sea was in that little vial, but everything in the little vial was the Dead Sea. The water was thick, oily, and about five times saltier than the ocean. The Dead Sea is the saltiest body of water on earth, about thirty percent solid. In a way, by gazing at this test tube of water, I had seen the Dead Sea.[1] And, analogously, when you look at Jesus, you are looking at God. "For in Christ all the fullness of the Deity lives in bodily form..."[2] When you look at Jesus, you are looking at "all the fullness of Deity" in a human container.

"...and you have been given fullness in Christ..."[3] It takes Him to complete you. There are multitudes of men and women who consider themselves to be Christians but have never yielded their life to Christ and invited Him to be their Lord and Savior. Curiously, if you look at the word CHRISTIAN - all spelled out - and eliminate the first syllable, CHRIST, you are left with just three letters: IAN. I'd guess that most churches have a lot more IANS (those without Christ) than CHRISTIANS. If you personally have never invited Jesus, through prayer, to be your Lord and Savior, then you must still be an IAN (a "Yin"). Remember that Jesus once said, "I am the vine; you are the branches...Apart from me you can do nothing."[4] IAN means "I-Am-Nothing." In other words, Without CHRIST, IAN. Without CHRIST, I AM NOTHING.

The New Testament scholar Warren Wiersbe shared his own personal experience. He said that, while waiting at the airport, he was accosted by a young man, I imagine in Hindu garb, who tried to sell him a book. Taking one look at its exotic cover, Wiersbe surmised that it was all about Eastern religion and philosophy. He interrupted his salesman, explaining that he happened to have in his briefcase a book of his own which met all his needs. He reached into it and produced a Bible. The young man quickly said, "Oh, we are not, in any way, opposed to your book. "It's just we've got something more which deepens our faith." His intended customer answered, " I don't need your 'something more'; There is nothing more I need than Jesus." At this, he began to flip the pages of his Bible to Colossians chapter 2, but by that time the young man was already down the corridor, searching for a more pliable customer. Then Warren Wiersbe went on to say that, sadly, there are many Christians who believe that they need something more: some guru, religious system, philosophy, some addendum. But in Jesus they already have everything they'll ever need.[5]

All you ever need is Jesus. Personally I look at it this way: if you take an eight-ounce glass and fill it to the very top, you can't add another drop. You can stand there and try to add another quart of water to the glass, but your glass is already full. You can't get fuller than full. That's just what Paul was emphasizing in his letter to these new Christians. "You are completely full in Him.

"...and you have been given fullness in Christ, who is the head over every power and authority."[6] At the end of Matthew's gospel, Jesus came to His followers and said, "All authority in heaven and on earth has been given to me."[7] And in Philippians we read: "Therefore God exalted him to the highest place and gave him the name that is above every name, that at the name of Jesus every knee should bow, in heaven and on earth and under the earth, and every tongue confess that Jesus Christ is Lord, to the glory of God the Father."[8]

I was thinking that whenever we give someone the gift of ourselves, we are giving a generous gift, no matter how miserably packaged we might happen to be. We are presenting them with "a gift that lasts a lifetime." But whenever we offer someone Jesus, we are giving them a gift that lasts through Eternity. One night I was in prayer when I seemed to hear a Voice speaking deeply to my soul. It said, "I have been waiting to minister through you, but you are so full of yourself that there's no room for Me. Move over, and let Me be Lord!" In the ensuing circumstances of life, I can still hear Him saying, "Move over, and let Me be Lord!"

Chapter 26: "Buried with Him...Raised in Him" (Col. 2:12 NIV)

Far back in the pages of the Old Testament, in the book of Genesis, we find this passage: "Then God said to Abraham, 'As for you, you must keep my covenant, you and your descendants after you for the generations to come...Every male among you shall be circumcised...and it will be the sign of the covenant between me and you.'"[1] A sign! Circumcision was therefore considered a physical sign that the male was in a right relationship with God.

But, two thousand years later, the Apostle Paul argued that a right relationship with God is really something not outward but inward. He expressed this to the Colossians when he wrote, "In [Christ] you were also circumcised, in the putting off of the sinful nature..."[2] In other words, a spiritual (not a physical) circumcision.

In the Old Testament, the Hebrew Bible, there were already signals from God that the true circumcision was to be spiritual. In Deuteronomy we read, "Circumcise you hearts, therefore, and do not be stiff-necked [stubborn] any longer."[3] Again, in Deuteronomy, "The Lord your God will circumcise your hearts and the hearts of your descendants, so that you may love him with all your heart and with all your soul, and live."[4] Not only Moses, but the great prophet Jeremiah also, saw the authentic circumcision as being spiritual rather than physical. So in Jeremiah we read, "...circumcise your hearts..."[5] To the Christians in the church in Rome Paul wrote, "A man is not a Jew if he is only one outwardly, nor is circumcision merely outward and physical. No, a man is a Jew if he is one inwardly; and circumcision is circumcision of the heart, by the Spirit, not by the written code."[6]

"In him you were also circumcised, in the putting off of the sinful nature, not with the circumcision done by the hands of men but with the circumcision done by Christ, having been buried with him in baptism and raised with him through your faith in the power of God, who raised him from the dead."[7] That's a big mouthful, but every word is like a drum-beat. Ralph Martin wrote that Paul, in the back of his mind, was picturing the baptism of believers in which the candidates first removed their clothes before entering the water.[8]

Symbolically the new converts were divesting themselves of their "old" self, ridding themselves of their old impulses and behavior.

In the New Testament, baptism was usually adult baptism and was by immersion.[9] I think that being immersed is like drowning, and rising out of the water is like new birth: being born out of the water of the womb. William Barclay described that thrilling moment for the baptismal candidates: They stepped down into the dark water, feeling it envelop and close over them - like death, like a burial. Then they emerged, saw the light all around them, and felt that they had just stepped into new life. They had repeated Jesus' death, burial, and resurrection.[10]

Elsewhere Paul wrote in his pastoral letter to the Romans: "Or don't you know that all of us who were baptized into Christ Jesus were baptized into his death? We were therefore buried with him through baptism into death in order that, just as Christ was raised from the dead through the glory of the Father, we too may live a new life."[11]

One of the most beautiful and inspiring passages in all of English literature comes from John Bunyan's The Pilgrim's Progress. In the course of the narrative we come to this scene: The narrator describes seeing it in a dream.

In his dream he sees a highway, walled in on either side. Christian, the pilgrim, has to travel on this road. It's a challenging pathway, made more difficult because he is running with a heavy burden on his back. As the road ascends he comes to a hill on which there stands a cross. Beneath it is a tomb. As our runner approaches this cross, the oppressive burden on his back suddenly slips away, rolls into the mouth of the open tomb, and disappears forever.[12]

A Passion hymn was written by Isaac Watts to which Ralph Hudson later added a chorus describing the joy of following Jesus:

"Alas! and did my Savior bleed.
And did my Sovereign die?
Would he devote that sacred head
For sinners such as I?

"At the cross, at the cross
Where I first saw the light,
And the burden of my heart
Rolled away;
It was there by faith
I received my sight,
And now I am happy all the day."[13]

Chapter 27: He Forgave Us" (Col. 2:13b NIV)

In an effort to demonstrate God's grace, Paul now proceeds to employ a series of images portraying His action in Christ.[1] Paul wrote, "When you were dead in your sins and in the uncircumcision of your sinful nature, God made you alive with Christ. He forgave us all our sins, having canceled the written code, with its regulation, that was against us, and that stood opposed to us;..."[2] That's a vivid picture of the sinner who has managed to dig a hole for himself. We each need to be rescued. And, just at the right moment, He did. He "made you alive with Christ"!

"He forgave us all our sins!" I remember a shameful episode from my own past. Actually, I could probably remember scores of shameful moments, but I'm trying to be selective here. I was a sixth grader at James Russell Lowell Elementary School in Philadelphia and had a teacher I dearly loved. Miss Eggly was devoted to her profession and labored mightily to motivate her students. One day, in the month of December, she announced, "I would like each of you to take a pencil and paper and write for me a Christmas story this morning." She wanted to test our spontaneous creative expression.

Well, all my classmates just sat there, nailed to their seats, looking puzzled and pensive. Around me I was aware that some were staring lethargically at their blank paper while others just sat there, twiddling their pencils or casually munching on an eraser. They were having a real problem with their assignment. In happy contrast, I had no problem at all. A Christmas story, hmm! I knew exactly what I would put down on my paper.

You see, the night before, my mother had asked me to read a story to my little six-year-old sister at bedtime. I selected a book and proceeded to read a lovely Christmas story about a nice family who took a walk in the woods, searching for the perfect Christmas tree. Now, sitting in Miss Eggly's classroom, I remembered that story with total recall. Almost unconsciously I began my own story (what I intended to be my own story) in the same setting. Gradually my story segued into the story I had just read. Oh, I hadn't planned to plagiarize. I guess I hoped that my plot would diverge from the original somewhere along the line. But it never happened. I wound up reproducing the story I had read in the book.

Now I looked triumphantly around the room. I could imagine all the other student enviously watching me, out of the corner of their eye, writing "fast and furious" as I filled up my paper. They, meanwhile, were struggling to put one word on top of another. I guessed that, so far, each had managed to crank out, "Once upon a time...," and now they were stuck. All their creative juice had run out (we hope not literally!). With a feeling of fulfillment, I turned in my paper.

That very night my conscience began to bother me. In an effort to "show up" my peer group, I figured I had cheated. All night long I tried to rationalize, but in my heart I knew. Theologians might say that I was "under conviction". The next day Miss Eggly handed back our marked papers. I was so hoping that she wouldn't say anything about mine, just pass it off as a mere handwriting exercise. But, no! She said, "Most of you didn't do too badly, but one of you wrote such a wonderful story it should be published." Unfortunately, it already had been. "Jerry Crossly, you really outdid yourself."

My fellow classmates glared at me with a mixture of jealousy and disdain. But all of their scorn, put together, could never match my own self-contempt. At lunchtime I approached my teacher. "Miss Eggly," I said, sheepishly. I couldn't ever bring myself to look at her. "What is it, Jerry?" I stammered, "That story I wrote wasn't really mine. I read it in a book." She looked at me with a deeply pained expression. "I'm very sorry!" was all she said. And I know in my heart that she somehow was sorry for both of us. Yet I also knew that she still loved me. I had been both loved and forgiven at the same time.

So it is with the Cross. We are judged and forgiven at the same time. "When you were dead in your sins and in the uncircumcision of your sinful nature, God made you alive with Christ. He forgave us all our sins..."[3] How many of your trespasses did He forgive? All of them.[4] One evangelist wrote that he often tells his students to make a list of their own sins, of all they've done that offends God. Then he tells them to call all their friends and invite them to add to that list all the sins they know he is guilty of. Then he mentions that, even if the Angel Gabriel happened to visit them with a much longer list, they needn't despair. He then reads to them this verse from Colossians 2:13: "He forgave us all our sins."[5]

Charles Wesley wrote one of Christendom's most beloved hymns:

> "O for a thousand tongues to sing
> My great redeemer's praise,
> The glories of my God and King,
> The triumphs of his grace!
>
> "Jesus! the name that charms our fears,
> That bids our sorrows cease;
> 'Tis music in the sinner's ears,
> 'Tis life, and health, and peace.
>
> "He breaks the power of canceled sin,
> He sets the prisoner free;
> His blood can make the foulest clean;
> His blood availed for me."[6]

Chapter 28: "Nailing It to the Cross" (Col 2:14b NIV)

"When you were dead in your sins..., God made you alive with Christ. He forgave us all our sins, having canceled the written code, with its regulations, that was against us and that stood opposed to us; he took it away, nailing it to the cross."[1] The Lord God looked at our record (and we all have one) and erased the evidence against us. He wiped the slate clean. In Isaiah the Lord says, "I, even I, am he who blots out your transgressions, for my own sake, and remembers your sins no more."[2]

In Jeremiah the Lord says, "The time is coming...when I will make a new covenant with the house of Israel and the house of Judah...I will put my law in their minds and write it on their hearts. I will be their God, and they will be my people...For I will forgive their wickedness and will remember their sins no more."[3] In Micah it is written, "You will again have compassion on us; you will tread our sins underfoot and hurl all our iniquities into the depths of the sea."[4]

And, finally, in the 103rd Psalm: "The Lord is compassionate and gracious, slow to anger, abounding in love. He will not always accuse, nor will he harbor his anger forever; he does not treat us as our sins deserve or repay us according to our iniquities. For as high as the heavens are above the earth, so great is his love for those who fear him: as far as the east is from the west, so far has he removed our transgressions from us. As a father has compassion on his children, so the Lord has compassion on those who fear him; for he knows how we are formed, he remembers that we are dust."[5]

Think about that image that is suggested: "As far as the east is from the west." I once heard some commentary on that, saying that if you travel north, around the globe, you'll eventually be going south. And if you go south, you'll reach a point on the globe, where you are going north. But if you go east, you'll never reach a point where you stop going east. And if you go west, you'll never stop going west. "As far as the east is from the west!" And we get the picture of a man's arms outstretched on a cross.

The 40th chapter of Isaiah begins a brand-new message. It's good news for the Hebrew captives. They had sinned grievously against the Lord, only to watch the armies of the Empire of Babylon destroy their precious Temple, demolish their Holy City, and decimate their population. Now the Lord was saying, "Comfort, comfort my people, says your God. Speak tenderly to Jerusalem; and proclaim to her that her hard service has been completed, that her sin has been paid for, that she has received from the Lord's hand double for all her sins."[6]

"Double"! What does that mean? Does that sound like a just God, punishing twice as much as one deserves? Had Judah, as a nation, been punished twice as much as she deserved? Actually, this is a picture of God's grace. Something much more beautiful is being proclaimed. Leslie Weatherhead explained it. In Old Testament times, if a person owed a debt and was in default, a sign might be posted in the marketplace, apprising every one of his debt. Thus, the debtor was publicly humiliated. Now, sometimes a sympathetic friend, seeing the sign, would voluntarily assume responsibility for the debt. He'd do this by removing the nail in the post, doubling over the posted notice, replacing the nail, and marking the accusation "Paid in full."

Therefore, when Isaiah wrote about God's people receiving "double" for all their sins, he might likely have been alluding to this custom. In that event, God had doubled over Judah's debts/sins and marked it "Paid in full."[7] Centuries later Jesus would go to the cross for each of us. His frail, fragile body would be doubled over on the cross, and the Lord God would write "Paid in full," signing it with Jesus' own blood.

He saw our sin and "took it away, nailing it to the cross."[8] Long ago the prophet Isaiah had written, "But he was pierced for our transgressions, he was crushed for our iniquities; the punishment that brought us peace was upon him, and by his wounds we are healed. We all, like sheep, have gone astray; each of us has turned to his own way; and the Lord has laid on him the iniquity of us all."[9] All of our sin - yours and mine - has been nailed to the cross.

I listened to the testimony of Corrie ten Boom, author of The Hiding Place. She and her pacifist family endeavored to live a quiet Christian life in her native Netherlands. Then, suddenly and without warning, a German blitzkrieg swept into her country like a torrent through a broken dike. Soon the S.S. were relentlessly rounding up Corrie's Jewish neighbors in the demonic "Final Solution". Corrie and her whole family risked their lives to protect them, providing, in their own home, a hiding place where the refugees might be safe. Eventually, being implicated as part of the Dutch Underground, the whole ten Boom family was arrested. Corrie later described a frightening moment during her interrogation.

She said that she was brought before a judge who held her life in the palm of his hand. And there was no doubt she was guilty. She mentioned that this was wartime, obliging her to do many things that warranted the death penalty. Yet somehow the Lord intervened, allowing Corrie to empathize with her inquisitor. She was moved by the Holy Spirit to offer her testimony, and the judge was visibly moved. Still he had his job to do.

He reached for a pack of papers that the Gestapo had discovered in her house. She was horrified to see the names, address, phone numbers, and personal information of family members and friends who were members of the Underground. The incriminating list sealed their fate. Her captor stared at her and asked, "Can you explain these papers?" She was unable to dodge the question. "Can you explain these papers?" "No, I can't," she answered. The judge knew very well what this damning evidence against her meant.

He turned, opened the door of the stove behind him, and threw the entire bundle of papers into the fire. She sat there, overjoyed. As the flames incinerated the evidence, she well-understood the words, "...he took it away, nailing it to the cross." Then she added that there are dangerous papers, evidence against us. They are there in Heaven. But if you know and have received Jesus as your personal Lord and Savior, you need not be afraid. Why not? Because the Lord has taken all that evidence and nailed it to the cross. In his beautiful hymn "It is Well with My Soul." Horatio Spafford wrote these lyrics;

"My sin, oh, the bliss of this glorious thought!

My sin, not in part but the whole,
Is nailed to the cross, and I bear it no more,
Praise the Lord, praise the lord, O my soul!"[10]

Chapter 29: "Triumphing" (Col. 2:15b NIV)

Here is a cry of victory: "And having disarmed the powers and authorities, he made a public spectacle of them, triumphing over them by the cross."[1] In other words, as Jesus hung upon the cross - vulnerable, vilified, defeated and disgraced - He "disarmed the power and authorities"[2] What amazing irony! What a miraculous reversal! God turned the tables on the powers that had put Jesus to death. When Jesus cried aloud, "It is finished,"[3] it was a cry not of dereliction, but of triumph. To every spectator that day, Jesus' ignominious ending looked simply like the death of a common criminal. Charles Wesley's timeless Easter hymn, "Christ the Lord is Risen Today," includes these words:

"Love's redeeming work is done,
Fought the fight, the battle won,
Alleluia!"[4]

The New Testament never denies the reality of the demonic. Instead, it claims that our Lord has conquered the dark side so that we don't have to be afraid of "things that go 'bump' in the night". Paul is telling his people that these evil, invisible powers, have been disarmed, that this spiritual time-bomb has been defused. A missionary related his personal experience of being in the presence of an unseen sinister power. He almost collapsed beneath the oppression and had no idea where to turn in order to escape its insidious clutches. He felt completely vulnerable. Then he remembered that there's power in Jesus' name, so he began to repeat it over and over. And whatever it was that had hold of him vanished, fleeing before the power of that name.[5]

"And having disarmed the powers and authorities, he made a public spectacle of them..."[6] Warren Wiersbe commented that every time a prominent Roman general scored a great victory, capturing treasures and hostages on foreign soil, the Empire would honor him and his returning troops with a homecoming parade known as "the Roman Triumph."[7] That vivid imagery was the mental picture that Paul had in mind. Just like the conquering Roman general, Jesus disarmed His supernatural enemies and led them captive in a triumphant procession.[8]

He disarmed them, "triumphing over them by the cross". In the fourth century A.D. there arose a new Emperor. Because he attempted to revive the former paganism of the Empire, he is called Julian the Apostate. Once, when his soldiers were tormenting a follower of Christ, one mockingly asked him, "So where is your 'Jesus the carpenter' now?" His victim answered, "He's building a coffin for your emperor." A few months later, Julian was fatally wounded in battle. As he lay dying he is reported to have said, 'You have conquered, O Galilean!" See, earthly kingdoms each have their day, and vanish. But His is the Kingdom forever and ever.[9] Far back in the Book of Daniel it is written, "His dominion is an everlasting dominion that will not pass away, and his kingdom is one that will never be destroyed."[10]

Now it occurs to me that all of this triumph is unseen; it's behind the scenes; it's behind the "seens". We cannot see it because it's occurring in the Supernatural, in a world of another dimension. "So we fix our eyes not on what is seen, but on what is unseen. For what is seen is temporary, but what is unseen is eternal."[11] What does this triumph mean for us? In one of my favorite passages of scripture, Romans 8, St. Paul wrote, "...in all these things we are more than conquerors through him who loved us. For I am convinced that neither death nor life, neither angels nor demons, neither the present nor the future, nor any powers, neither height nor depth, nor anything else in all creation, will be able to separate us from the love of God that is in Christ Jesus our Lord."[12]

Chapter 30: "The Reality...is Found in Christ" (Col. 2:17b NIV)

The Colossians had just been reading about all that Jesus had endured, and all that He had achieved for them. It was now time to introduce a cautionary note: "Therefore do not let anyone judge you by what you eat or drink, or with regard to a religious festival, a New Moon celebration of a Sabbath Day. These are a shadow of the things that were to come; the reality, however, is found in Christ."[1] He was saying, in effect, "Look, Jesus has already died for your sins. So don't let other people hassle you with a whole bunch of legalisms. Our Christian faith is more than a religion of dos' and don'ts; it's about relationship." Paul was attacking bad religion.[2]

Don't let anyone judge you about what you eat or what you drink. In Mark's gospel we find this encounter: "Again Jesus called the crowd to him and said, 'Listen to me, everyone, and understand this. Nothing outside a man can make him 'unclean' by going into him. Rather it is what comes out of a man that makes him 'unclean'. For from within, out of men's hearts, come evil thought, sexual immorality, theft, murder, adultery, greed, malice, deceit, lewdness, envy, slander, arrogance, and folly. All these evils come from inside and make a man 'unclean'."[3]

When I served as a volunteer chaplain at Holmesburg Prison in Philadelphia, I had many conversations with the inmates. I was in the section where men were awaiting trial for crimes committed for drugs or while on drugs. Without exception, they blamed all their crimes on drugs themselves. They worked overtime to convince me that they were wonderful guys, but it was just these drugs and alcohol that prompted them to commit the crime. They backed away from admitting any responsibility. They figured that the evil came from the outside, rather than from the inside. To connect sin with food and drink is to misunderstand the real nature of sin. Elsewhere the Apostle wrote, "For the kingdom of God is not a matter of eating and drinking, but of righteousness, peace and joy in the Holy Spirit..."[4]

Years ago my wife Julie and I attended a three-day conference for pastors and their wives. We listened to nationally-known evangelical speakers discourse about the foundations of our faith.

Most of the ministers attending that conference pastored independent fundamental churches. Upon meeting us, they would proudly announce, "I am the pastor of something-or-other Independent Bible Church," or, "I am the pastor of Living Faith Pulpit Banging Fellowship Church, Inc." Then they would casually ask, "What church do you represent?"

I'd answer, "A little Methodist Church." "Methodist?" they'd harumph. "What are you doing here? "Indignantly, I'd answer, "The same thing you are doing here." See, the independent pastors were suspicious of any mainline denomination church, which they assumed has a more liberal theology than they could tolerate. Any pastors or laity representing those congregations were unworthy of their warm and friendly fellowship. My wife and I felt rejected, unclean, leprous. A little legalism goes a long way.

And don't let anyone judge you in regard to a religious festival, a New Moon celebration of a Sabbath day.[5] My first thought is, "What in the world is he talking about?" Well, as I thought about it, we wonder how to observe Sunday. Can we do any work on that day? Can I mow the lawn or pull weeds? If we decide to go to a restaurant, aren't we obliging the cook, the cashier, the waitress and the hostess to work for us? Once Jesus said, "The Sabbath was made for man, not man for the Sabbath."[6] In other words, it's not the worship of the Sabbath that finally counts, but the worship of the Lord of the Sabbath.

All these mandatory observances "are a shadow of the things that were to come; the reality, however, is found in Christ."[7] To simplify what I think Paul meant, here's an analogy. Suppose you were enroute to visit someone you had never visited before. You were told that this individual lived on "Conestoga Street". You kept searching for your destination. Finally you discovered a street sign saying, "Conestoga Street." You were ecstatic. You congratulated yourself that you had arrived. In reality you hadn't. You were only at the street sign pointing towards your destination. So everything in the Bible is basically the street sign pointing towards Him. It isn't till you actually come to Jesus that you have arrived. All you ever need is Jesus.

In his profound book, Evidence That Demands a Verdict, Josh McDowell shared his testimony. When he entered his university as a college student, he was a convinced agnostic. However, he soon became aware of a small group of students, and a couple of professors, who were noticeably different in the way they thought, lived, and behaved. They were completely calm amidst the storms of life that would have shattered others. They harbored an inner peace and joy. Josh McDowell envied them because he did not personally have any of this. So he began to question them about what they believed, and why.

He asked them what it was that seemed to make them so different. One young woman looked him straight in the eye and said, "Jesus." He contemptuously scoffed. "Oh, don't give me that stuff. Don't talk to me about religion. I've had more than enough of 'religion'." She shot back, "Did I say 'religion'? I didn't say anything about 'religion', did I?! I said 'Jesus'." She then went on to explain that authentic Christianity isn't a 'religion'. Religion is all about people trying to climb up to God. Christianity is about God coming down to men and women, offering them a relationship with Himself.

Josh MCowell later wrote that on December 29, 1959, at 8:30 p.m. he became a Christian. Someone asked him, "How do you know all this was real?" He answered, "I know. I was there. It changed my life."[8]

Chapter 31: "Do Not Let Anyone Disqualify You" (Col. 2:18 NIV)

Whenever we reflect upon our own sporadic loss of spirituality and commitment to Christ, we are prone to count ourselves out as genuine Christians. But Paul wrote to the Colossians, "Do not let anyone...disqualify you..."[1] I suppose he meant "including yourself". He was using a term from the field of sports in which a referee could arbitrarily disqualify a contender because of an infraction of the rules.[2] So he was saying, "Don't let any umpire disqualify you because he thought you weren't properly following the rules."[3] By one bad call, the umpire could deprive a contender the prize he had earned.[4]

Look, there are always going to be those people who are ready to count you out because they think that you're not saved, or perhaps you're not saved enough. Our first two churches were in the Pocono mountains of Pennsylvania. There, "on top of the mountain", there was a peculiar history of church splits. It began with one group of disgruntled (notice that we talk about "disgruntled" people; we never talk about people who are only "gruntled") parishioners who left our Methodist churches because we obviously weren't saved.

They drew their righteous skirts around themselves and formed a Holiness Church. This of course was a fellowship of the twice-born (whereas we were stuck with our once-born kids!). But then, some of the members of this new congregation felt that they hadn't gone far enough in expurgating sin, worldliness, and just plain wrong-thinking. So they split and formed a new Bible Fellowship Church. They were the authentic community of the redeemed - until some of them decided that their former community was somehow contaminated. Curiously, each group decided that it was "more saved". Well, you can't get "more saved" than "saved".

"Do not let anyone who delights in false humility and the worship of angels disqualify you for the prize."[5] What's this "angels" stuff? Angels were considered very powerful and supernatural. Those who experienced their presence wound up feeling very superior to those who lacked that revelation.[6] But the fact was that the worship of angels began to take the focus off Jesus. It derailed the worshipers; it threw them off track.[7] It's like falling in love with love instead of falling in love with a person. We are not saved by angels; we're saved by Jesus. The author of Hebrews announced, "So he [Jesus] became as much superior to the angels as the name he has inherited is superior to theirs. For to which of the angels did God ever say, 'You are my son...'?"[8]

People were imagining that angels were the mediators between us and God, and that only through them could we approach Him.[9] Yet in 1 Timothy we read, "For there is one God and one mediator between God and men, the man Christ Jesus, who gave himself as a ransom for all..."[10] It is He who once said, "I am the gate; whoever enters through me will be saved."[11] This is why I appreciated the words of the hymn "Spirit of God, Descend Upon My Heart."

"I ask no dream, no prophet ecstasies,
No Sudden rending of the veil of clay,
No angel visitant, no opening skies,
But take the dimness of my soul away."[12]

The Lord wants us to grow not in ourselves - puffed up and proud - but in Him. He has told us in John 15 that He's the vine and we are the branches.[13] That surely means that we are "no good if detached". How do we grow? By staying close to the trunk. One morning I went to a local nursery to purchase a shrub or tree that might beautify our property. I wanted to display it prominently in our garden. A golden-threaded cypress (or something like that) caught my eye. It was an evergreen with delicate, lacy branches. It was beautiful. I asked the manager of the nursery, "Will it grow?" "If you plant it in the soil, it's going to grow." He was right. Today it's as big as our house.

Plant it in the soil. We will grow if we are planted and deeply rooted in the rich soil of His Word. We might fantasize "branching out", but we are not going to branch out if we are not rooted. Remember, we have to grow down before we grow up. The Apostle Peter offered all of us a benediction: "But grow in the grace and knowledge of our Lord and Savior Jesus Christ. To him be glory both now and forever! Amen."[14]

Chapter 32: "As Though You Still Belonged to [this World]" (Col. 2:20 NIV)

Here's a burning question that Paul is posing: "Since you died with Christ to the basic principles of this world, why, as though you still belonged to it, do you submit to its rules?"[1] Why are you continuing to allow yourself to be dominated by the world? You're never going to know who you are until you realize Whose you are. The people of the church in Colossae were being told that you shouldn't do this or that, eat this or that, taste or touch this or that. Observing all these man-made rules might make you feel self-righteous and superior, but it took you away from God. So Paul attacked this asceticism.

Warren Wiersbe noted that those who practice self-denial, and even self-mortification, imagine that they are becoming more spiritual. They believe that they are closer to God. Wiersbe reminded us that in the Middle Ages there were those ascetics who deliberately wore hair shirts, flagellated themselves with whips, and tormented their bodies to bring them greater righteousness.[2] None of this comes close to tempting me. It all sounds weird. It's like being issued an invitation to slide down a razor blade (and I am already a split-personality).

This discussion reminds me of an old joke about a young woman who joined a religious order and entered a convent where silence was the rule. Once, every ten years, the nuns were permitted to address the Mother Superior and express herself with a handful of words. For ten years this nun faithfully observed the law of silence. At last, when she was allowed to speak, she looked at the Mother Superior and said, "Bed too hard." That's all she said, and for the next ten years lived in total silence.

Then, after twenty years had passed by her golden opportunity came around again. She came to the Mother Superior and said, "Food too cold," then walked away for another ten years-worth of silence. Finally, after thirty years, she once more approached the Mother Superior and exclaimed, "I quit!" "Good!" said the Mother Superior." You've done nothing but complain since your got here."

(I'd like to footnote this story, but no one will take the responsibility.)

Is seems to me that asceticism, in general, is an exercise in futility. It's self-defeating. When we struggle to deny ourselves, we wind up being more aware of ourselves than ever. There are many would-be followers of Jesus who have a negative religion. They excessively take pride in what they don't do instead of what they do. Are there some things we should deprive ourselves of? Sure. We should deprive ourselves of hatred, prejudice, demeaning others, despising and disrespecting those whom we want to marginalize or reject. We might proudly say to the Lord, "you're lucky to have me. I don't drink, smoke, dance, wear toenail polish, or vape." And maybe the Lord says, "But what do you do?"

Paul said that all these "regs" and rules are bound to perish because they're based on man-made commands and teachings.[3] But behind all of them is a much higher law: God's law of love. "A new command I give you: Love one another. As I have loved you, so you must love one another. By this all men will know that you are my disciples, if you love one another."[4] Where did His followers learn to be loving? By watching Jesus.

Once there was a senior director of a prominent bank in New York City. He had climbed the ladder of success in his profession to become a highly-respected executive. What was extraordinary was the way it had all begun. He had started his climb at the very bottom. He was an office boy. Whatever task he was given, he did. Now, one day the bank president summoned the young man into his office. "Listen, son, I want you to come into my office each day and work here by my side. I need you always to be available."

The startled office boy exclaimed, "But how can I be of any worthwhile assistance to you, sir? I don't know anything about finance and investments and all those things." "That's quite alright. You don't have to know all this initially. You're going to learn faster everything you need to know if you just stick with me. Watch and listen to everything I say and do."

The man telling this story, the man who was now the senior director, said, "That was the most critical event of my life. For as I observed him and listened to him, I actually became like him. I could anticipate what he would say and what he would do. I myself began to do all those things, utilizing his methods and approach." In just the same way, we can be changed and transformed by keeping our eyes on Christ Jesus.[5] Just keep close to Him and then keep your eyes and ears open.

Chapter 33: "Set our Hearts on Things Above: (Col. 3:1 NIV)

We come to the third chapter of Paul's letter, and it is a watershed. In the first two chapters he endeavors to provide correctives to their theology because several distortions have appeared, causing them to veer off course. Chapter 3 begins with these words, "Since, then, you have been raised with Christ..."[1] In other words, since you have been saved by His grace, then it follows that your life is going to have to change. Chapter 3 thus begins the practical applications of this belief.[2] How are they going to apply their new-found faith to their daily living? What follows when you put your life "under new management"?

Fritz Ridenour writes that we have the same problem today: how to be a Christian in an un-Christian world.[3] Many of us tend to forget that the Christian faith is more than a belief system; it's a whole way of life that embraces every aspect of our daily life. Remember what those first Christians were called before they were called "Christians"? They were known as followers of the "way". I like that. The fact that they were defined by this phrase indicates that they saw their faith as a whole way of life.

Paul said that followers of Christ Jesus had already been "raised".[4] In Ephesians we read, "But because of his great love for us, God, who is rich in mercy, made us alive with Christ even when we were dead in transgressions - it is by grace you have been saved. And God raised us up with Christ and seated us with him in the heavenly realms..."[5]

"Since, then, you have been raised with Christ, set your hearts on things above, where Christ is seated at the right hand of God. Set your minds on things above, not on earthly things."[6] Dwight L. Moody believed that much of a burden a Christian carries is comprised of stuff that he imagines are harmless. He illustrated this very picturesquely in a worship service.

Bent beneath a heavy backpack, he limped slowly across the platform, then said to his curious audience, "Do you believe that I am fully free to preach with this burden on my back?" They didn't think so. Then he added that most of the stuff in his backpack consisted of harmless things. These harmless things happened to be holding him back. Moody's point was that it is the so-called "harmless" obsessions that prevent us from living fully. We need to drop these extra weights so that we can leave them behind and embrace the life to which we have been called.[7]

A balloonist was relating his first experience in flying a hot air balloon. When he examined it, he was surprised to see that the whole perimeter of the gondola was draped with sandbags. It occurred to him that as these bags, acting as ballast, are released, the hot air balloon will begin to rise. Then he saw the analogy. As a Christian, the more ballast he could get rid of in his own life, the closer he would rise to God.[8]

In Hebrews we read, "Therefore, since we are surrounded by such a great cloud of witnesses, let us throw off everything that hinders and the sin that so easily entangles, and let us run with perseverance the race marked out for us. Let us fix our eyes on Jesus, the author and perfector of our faith, who for the joy set before him endured the cross, scorning its shame, and sat down at the right hand of the throne of God."[9]

Some creatures, including us humans, find it difficult to impossible to abandon their this-worldly pursuits. One day it happened that a lovely swan glided down from the sky and alighted next to a crane who was completely focused on finding snails. He was standing in the oozing mud of a swamp, searching for his dinner. "Well hello!" he said to the swan. "I didn't see you. Where did you come from?" "Heaven", answered the swan. "Heaven? I never heard of such a place. What's it like?" The swan replied, "You mean to me that you've never heard of streets of gold and gates of pearl?" "Never. But, tell me, does it have a lot of snails?" "No, it doesn't", answered the swan. "Then", said the crane, "You can keep your Heaven. I'll stick with my snails." And that's true of many people who would prefer to forego the prospect of Heaven and stick to their own version of snails.[10]

Fanny Crosby, the blind poet who blesses us with so many touching hymns, wrote:

"Take the world, but give me Jesus;
All its joys are but a name,
But His love abideth ever,
Thro' eternal years the same.

"Take the world, but give me Jesus;
In His cross my trust shall be,
Till, with clearer, brighter vision,
Face to face my Lord I see."[11]

Chapter 34:"Your Life in Now Hidden with Christ" (Col. 3:3 NIV)

"Set your minds on things above, not on earthly things. For you died, and your life is now hidden with Christ in God."[1] You have died to self. Warren Wiersbe told about two sisters who apparently were "party girls". I suppose that, if there was a party anywhere anytime, they'd be sure to be there. One day they had an encounter with Christ, a "come to Jesus" experience and the whole direction of their life changed.

Afterwards, they received an RSVP invitation to a gala party, the sort of occasion which, in the past, they would have relished. Now they were no longer interested. So they responded with these words, "We are very sorry that we will be unable to attend because we just recently died."[2] I'm sure that their reply puzzled its recipient, but the sisters meant that they had died to their former behavior and life-style so that they could new life in Christ Jesus.

"For you died, and your life is now hidden with Christ in God."[3] It's as if Paul were saying, "Look, no one can ever rob you of your soul because it's safely locked away in Heaven." You did not take your life and waste it. Instead, you invested it in the Kingdom of Heaven where it's safely locked away, like money in the bank. Whatever is deposited with God can never be lost or destroyed.

"Your life is now hidden with Christ in God." Long ago, in the incomparably beautiful 27th Psalm, the poet wrote, "For in the day of trouble he will keep me safe in his dwelling; he will hide me in the shelter of his tabernacle and set one high upon a rock...The Lord is my light and my salvation - whom shall I fear? The Lord is the stronghold of my life - of whom shall I be afraid?"[4]

A certain monarch summoned his subject into his exalted presence and demanded that he renounce his Christian faith. If not, he would be exiled, banished from his home. He wasn't intimidated. "You can separate me from my home but not from my Lord. He has promised that He will never leave nor forsake us." The king grew angrier. "If you don't do as I command, I will confiscate all that you own." His subject replied, "It's alright. All my treasure is laid up in Heaven." Furious, the king announced, "I am going to impose the death penalty." The man said, with assurance, "My life is hid with Christ."[5]

Paul then made this promise to the Colossians: "When Christ, who is your life, appears, then you also will appear with him in glory."[6] Once Jesus said, "...men will see the Son of Man coming in clouds with great power and glory."[7] A mother who was very, very pregnant continued with her little burden for a very, very long time. The ninth month passed, and the big question was, "When will this little person make its appearance?" The child frustrated everybody's predictions. But, undeniably, he was on his way. It did not matter how late he might arrive; he was going to arrive in his own time."[8]

A little boy was sitting on the living room floor, happily playing with his toys, when he observed the tall, old grandfather clock in the corner of the room. It was ticking noisily and almost noon. He knew that when both hands pointed at "12", then the chimes would begin to ring. At noon the clock began chiming, and the little boy counted each gong. However, something misfired in the clock's mechanism, and the chimes continued to ring: "13, 14, 15, 16". The little boy could not believe what was happening or why. He leapt to his feet and ran toward the kitchen, all the while shouting, "Grandma! Grandma! It's later than it's ever been before!"[9] And he's right, more right than he ever suspected.

"When Christ, who is your life, appears, then you also will appear with him in glory.[10] That's His promise to those who put their trust in Him. Once He said, "Whoever serves me must follow me; and where I am, my servant will also be."[11] And He said, "Before long, the world will not see me anymore but you will see me. Because I live, you also will live."[12] Quoting the prophet Isaiah, Paul wrote, "No eye has seen, nor ear has heard, no mind has conceived what God has prepared for those who love him."[13]

We can trust in that promise. There well might be terrible circumstances that will confront us ahead. Like every human being on this earth, Christians face the threats of disease, disaster, death, bereavement and a host of other ills. But we carry in our heart the assurance that, somehow, we are hidden in, and enveloped by, God's love. And that faith is all-sufficient.

Chapter 35: "The Life You Once Lived" (Col. 3:7 NIV)

"Put to death, therefore, whatever belongs to your earthly nature..."[1] Paul was referring to all the stuff that springs up impulsively from our primal nature: our passions and uncontrollable desires.[2] Whatever stands between you and the Lord get rid of. You know what it is. In His Sermon on the Mount, Jesus said, "If your right eye causes you to sin, gouge it out and throw it away. It is better for you to lose one part of your body than for your whole body to be thrown into hell. And if your right hand causes you to sin, cut it off and throw it away. It is better for you to lose one part of your body than for your whole body to go into hell."[3] Do whatever it takes to detach yourself from self-destructive behavior.

To the Christians in the church in Rome, Paul wrote,"...don't you know that all of us who were baptized into Christ Jesus were baptized into his death? We were therefore buried with him through baptism into death in order that, just as Christ was raised from the dead through the glory of the Father, we too may live a new life.[4] In the same way, count yourselves dead to sin but alive to God in Christ Jesus."[5]

At this point in his letter, Paul is about to enumerate a long list of sins. His list isn't meant to be exhaustive; instead, the list is representative. It seems to me that all our little sins actually originate in one big sin: our incorrigible self-centeredness. An old preacher once quipped, "Sin is going to carry you further than you meant to go, keep you longer than you meant to stay and charge you much more than you meant to pay."[6]

When temptations appear in your life, don't welcome them and make them feel at home. J. Vernon McGee offered this helpful illustration. He was relating how often someone will show up for counseling, in the course of which they will reveal a sin that they've committed. "Why did you do it?" "I don't know. I just couldn't help myself." The pastor feels that the counselee has deliberately put themselves in a situation in which they might be tempted.

Stop doing that! He told about a little boy who, one night, was rummaging in the kitchen. He had already discovered and opened the very inviting cookie jar. His mother suspected that he was "up to no good". "What are you doing in there?" The little boy replied, "I am trying my best to overcome temptation." J. Vernon McGee concluded that, if you really want to overcome temptation, you should not hang around the cookie jar![7]

God's wrath is aroused by our missteps.[8] I think that we persist so energetically in picturing a warm, loving Father God who tolerates anything and everything, that we cannot imagine Him becoming angry. His love and His "righteous indignation" appear to be incongruous. Yet love and judgment are two sides of the same coin.[9] Judgment without love is oppressive; love without judgment is permissive. I think God's wrath is not against the sinner as much as it is against the sin that has ensnared him. A genuinely just and loving person will feel wrathful towards apartheid, genocide, inequality, terrorism, violations of human dignity. Even so, God's wrath is an expression of outraged love.

Paul summarizes, "You used to walk in these ways in the life you once lived."[10] Personally, I think that in each Christian's life there should be a "B.C." (before Christ) and a "A.D." (Anno Domini, the year of our Lord). After the Lord came into my own life, it changed. We cannot stay the same. If we really take Jesus seriously then our life cannot be "business as usual".

A prosperous and prominent Englishman paid a visit to the Fiji Islands and was given a private interview with the tribal chief. The tourist complimented him on the islands' cultural and material progress, but then apologized for the foreign missionaries who came and paternalistically labored to change their behaviors and lifestyle and belief system. The English visitor considered them to be manipulative and exploitive.

The tribal chieftain totally disagreed with him and said, "Do you see that large rock over there? That's where we used to bring intruders who we captured. We'd bring them here and smash their heads. And see that pit over there? That's where we would barbecue them. If it hadn't been for those missionaries with their Bibles and stories of Jesus, we'd still be practicing cannibalism on our tourists. And you, sir, would not be an honored guest; you'd be dinner."[11]

Chapter 36: "Put on the New Self" (Col. 3:10 NIV)

All of us carry a lot of "baggage" from our past. We know that. What do we do about it? We get rid of it. We dump it. The author of Hebrews wrote, "Therefore, since we are surrounded by such a great cloud of witnesses, let us throw off everything that hinders and the sin that so easily entangles, and let us run with perseverance the race marked out for us."[1] St. Paul is delivering that same message to the Colossians: "But now you must rid yourselves of all such things as these: anger, rage, malice, slander, and filthy language from your lips."[2] Don't drag into your new life in Christ all the old garbage of your life. Dump it!

Paul goes on to say, "Do not lie to each other, since you have taken off your old self with its practices and have put on the new self, which is being renewed in knowledge in the image of its Creator."[3] Paul is now painting a word picture of a Believer's Baptism. The person being baptized took off his old clothes and put on new clothes (as he emerged from the water), thus symbolizing a renunciation of a former lifestyle and replacement with a brand-new lifestyle.[4] He came out of the water and put on a new, pure white robe. He was stepping into a new life.[5] The act of a Believer's Baptism carried the message that "We too may live a new life."[6]

So before we "put on", we must "put off". Rabbi David A. Nelson told a story about two brothers who had been feuding with one another for years. They each wanted to resolve those issues of the past, so they went to their rabbi for a little assistance. He listened carefully, eventually arranging a reconciliation. He asked them to shake hands. Then, as they were about to take their leave of the rabbi and each other, the rabbi invited them each to make a wish for the other, to honor and celebrate the Jewish New Year. The first brother turned to his sibling and said, cryptically, "I am wishing for you what you are wishing for me." The second brother immediately turned to the rabbi and whined, "Listen to him! He's starting the whole thing up again."[7]

Paul talked about ridding ourselves of malice and slander. A woman, whose personal life was rather dull and monotonous, suddenly began to receive cards and gifts from someone who signed her name "Secret Pal". Every special occasion - from a birthday to holidays - were enhanced by the remembrances sent by her "Secret Pal". At the same time all this was happening, this woman was entertaining a deep hatred for a woman she knew, growing more and more hostile and malicious.

Then, one day, this woman she could not tolerate died. Her sense of civility led her to visit the family of the woman she had detested for years. As she was sitting there in that woman's home, she saw an unmailed letter sitting there, with her own name and address on the envelope. In one shocking, painful moment of truth, she realized that this woman whom she secretly hated had been her Secret Pal. And now it was too late to make amends.[8] Because of Jesus, we have to be through with that kind of behavior. We have to dump it and move on.

"Put on the new self." For almost five years I came to Holmesburg Prison in Philadelphia as a chaplain. I was assigned to work in the drug unit, a portion of the prison for about fifteen young men in their twenties who had committed drug-related offenses. In other words, they had either committed a crime while on drugs, under their influence, or else they had committed a crime in order to obtain drugs. There were two female social workers assigned to our unit. Privately the inmates confided to me that they would master the nomenclature used by the social workers, and then simply play it back to them. In this way they would dupe the counselors into imagining that they (both inmates and counselors) were making progress. In reality, they were being blind-sided. The inmates persisted in their devious behavior but remained untouched and unchanged.

My good friend Nick Barbetta, a "gold star chaplain" in the prison system, had once been a big-time drug dealer in Florida, until Jesus changed his life. Nick said to me, "Sociologists will never change these guys. It's like taking the Prodigal Son out of the pigpen, giving him a bath, dressing him up, and then letting him go right back into the pigpen. Only Jesus can change them!"

In 2 Corinthians we find this announcement: "Therefore, if anyone is in Christ, he is a new creation: the old has gone, the new has come!"⁹ Remember those classic words of wisdom: "Your life is God's gift to you. What you do with it is your gift back to God."¹⁰

Chapter 37: "Clothe Yourselves" (Col. 3:12 NIV)

Here's a big question for you: What should a Christian wear? People generally spend an inordinate amount of time deciding what they should be wearing. I looked at old photographs from churches in the 1950s. Almost all the women in those congregations were wearing hats. Maybe it was mandatory. Styles change so fast so that you will feel obligated to purchase the "latest" in order to be in style. Honestly, what you wear on your body is not as important as what you are wearing on your heart. "Therefore, as God's chosen people, holy and dearly loved, clothe yourselves with compassion, kindness, humility, gentleness and patience."[1] That's it. That's your wardrobe.

The Lord is calling each of us His chosen people. That's certainly an attention-getter. Remember that this message is being delivered to Gentiles. The Lord God has summoned the Jews to be His chosen people; now He's inviting the Gentiles to join them.[2] Peter wrote these words which reinforce God's gracious invitation: "But you are a chosen people, a royal priesthood, a holy nation, a people belonging to God, that you may declare the praise of him who called you out of darkness into his wonderful light. Once you were not a people, but now you are the people of God; once you had not received mercy, but now you have received mercy."[3]

"Therefore, as God's chosen people, holy and dearly loved, clothe yourselves with compassion..."[4] That's your first article of new clothing. One intensely hot, oppressive morning, two workers were laboring to paint a farmhouse. They saw a young boy approaching them on a bicycle. As he came closer, they noticed that he was missing one arm. He rode up to them and said, "My mom wants to know if you'd like something cold to drink. If you do, I can go and fetch it for you."

The younger worker did not want this very accommodating young boy, pedaling a bike with only one arm, to go to any trouble for them. So he was just about to say, "It's really O.K. We brought our own water supply." He never had the chance to say it because his older partner quickly intervened, "You showed up just in time. We could really use a cold drink." The young boy lit up with a big smile. "I'll be right back. I bet you all felt lucky that I showed up!" "That's for sure," said the older worker. "We don't have to worry now that we've got another man to help us out!" Years later the young worker commented on what had transpired in that encounter. He said, "With just a handful of words, my fellow worker had managed to transform a seriously handicapped boy into a confident young man.[5] That's a lesson in compassion.

Then put on kindness. And add humility. Fritz Ridenour discussed his urge to write a book about "Christian Humility and How I attained It."[6] Humility tends to be a forgotten virtue. I once heard that genuine humility is not about thinking poorly of yourself; instead, it's about not thinking of yourself at all. And add gentleness and patience. J. Vernon McGee said that he had written a sermon on Colossians 3:12 and entitled it, "What the Well-Dressed Christian Will Wear This Year".[7]

Remember again how the Apostle Peter wrote, "But you are a chosen people, a royal priesthood, a holy nation, a people belonging to God, that you may declare the praises of him who called you out of darkness into his wonderful light."[8] Christians in the twenty first century? Dress for the part!

Chapter 38: "Put on Love" (Col. 3:14 NIV)

"Therefore, as God's chosen people...Bear with each other..."[1] That's a challenge. It's tough to bear with people who happen to be unbearable. Why is it that it's so much easier to love from afar but not close-up and personal? I, long ago, learned that many people who claim to "love everybody" seem to have difficulty loving anybody. Yet here is St. Paul telling us that we must "bear with each other". Maybe that's why he's a saint!

It reminds me of a little story. One day a laborer was busy spreading cement on a pavement. Just as he finished, a mischievous child appeared and ran through the cement. The distressed worker shouted at him and then proceeded to re-do the sidewalk. Once again, just as he had finished, the little boy materialized and practically performed a Spanish Flamenco dance through the wet pavement. Once again the disgusted worked yelled at the young intruder. Across the street, a front door opened, and the child's upset mother stood on the porch. "What's the matter with you, mister? Don't you like little boys?" To which he answered, "Madam, I like little boys in the abstract but not in the concrete!" Come to think of it, that's how most of us like other people. But Paul says, "Bear with each other."

Then Paul said, "...forgive whatever grievances you may have against one another."[2] There's no use of our re-visiting the past to examine who was at fault. We all have a propensity to do that. We want to scrutinize the past with slow-motion instant replay. But what good does that ever do? It cannot change anything. Dump it and go on. Genuine forgiveness means saying, "What's past is past, but where do we go from here?"

One man said to Rev. John Wesley, "I make it a rule never to forgive." Wesley responded, "Then I hope, sir, that you never sin."[3] How terrible it is to live with unforgiveness. I recalled a story about two literary giants. Williams Thackeray and Charles Dickens were both suffering from professional jealousy and rivalry. They quarreled. Then, in 1863, just before Christmas, the two men bumped into one another in London. They refused to speak. As they walked away from each other, Thackeray's conscience ached.

He turned around, reached out and grabbed the hand of his former friend, saying, "I can't stand this estrangement between us." Charles Dickens, deeply moved by this open gesture of reconciliation, gratefully allowed all his old grievances to melt away. Eagerly, he restored their friendship. Not long afterwards, Thackeray died. A mutual friend later wrote that when he next saw Dickens, the author was standing reverently at the grave of his former rival. But he must have had the memory of that handshake and the joy of the renewal of their genuine affection.[4]

Leonardo da Vinci, who excelled in so many disciplines, was poised to launch into a project destined to create one of the world's most inspiring and enduring works of art: "The Last Supper". However, just before he began, he engaged in a violent argument with a fellow artist. Infuriated, he thought of a sinister way to avenge himself. In painting the face of Judas, he would use the face of his enemy. No matter who looked at the resulting portrait, they would recognize this man who would live on in infamy.

Leonardo painted the face of Judas almost at the beginning of his work. Yet, when it came time to paint the face of Christ, he couldn't do it. He did not understand why, and made many futile attempts. Something stood in his way. Suddenly he knew what it was: his own hatred. He had copied his enemy's face and used it as the face of Judas. That is why he could not paint the face of Christ. So he painted out that face of Judas and began to paint Jesus. This time he succeeded and created an artistic masterpiece that continues to inspire.[5] Until we see the face of our brother and our sister, we'll never see the face of Christ.

"Forgive as the Lord forgave you."[6] Sometimes we piously say that we have forgiven. We claim that we have forgiven, but then we'll add, emphatically, "I'll never have anything more to do with him/her." One woman once expressed that sentiment to an evangelist, who responded, "Is that how you want the Lord to treat you? Do you want Him to forgive you and then say to you, "I forgive you, but I never want anything more to do with you!"[7] Repeat after me: "Forgive as the Lord forgave you."

All of us love "the Lord's Prayer".⁸ Roman Catholics call it "the Our Father", and that's probably correct because the prayer that Jesus prayed Himself is in John chapter 17. We tend to rattle it off by rote, praying, "And forgive us our debts/trespasses, as we forgive our debtors/those who trespass against us." We sort of lose sight of the fact we are praying "as we forgive". Then there's something else we forget. Immediately following the prayer, Jesus said, "For if you forgive [others[when they sin against you, your heavenly Father will also forgive you. But if you do not forgive [others] their sins, your Father will not forgive your sins."⁹

Then Paul added a key phrase, "And over all these virtues put on love..."¹⁰ Remember that Paul is talking about garments we should put on like new clothes. We cherish the "love chapter" in 1 Corinthians. There we read about a love like God's: constant, selfless, unconditional. The Apostle Paul put it this way: "If I speak in the tongues of men and of angels, but have not love, I am only a resounding gong or a clanging cymbal. If I have the gift of prophecy and can fathom all mysteries and all knowledge, and if I had a faith that can move mountains, but have not love, I gain nothing."¹¹

"Put on love, which binds them [all these virtues] together in perfect unity."¹² What did he mean by that? A Bible scholar, W.H. Griffith Thomas, offered the following explanation. He pointed out that Paul was using clothing and dressing up as his imagery. In the Middle East, a belt or girdle or waistband is used to hold one's robe, and other articles of clothing, together. In the same way, love holds together all the other virtues to make one ensemble.¹³

I grew up in a little church in the Oak Lane neighborhood of Philadelphia;. All my buddies attended this church with me, and my mother taught the "Ladies Bible Class". There were many aspects of that church that were mysterious to me. I didn't understand the mechanics of the local church government or the faith that everyone seemed to share. But I understood one thing. Those people really cared about me and all the rest of the young people. I experienced their unconditional love and acceptance.

Years later, when I was away at college, I was sorely tempted to throw away the whole Christian faith, heritage, and tradition. Only one thing stopped me: the genuine love of all those who held that faith dear. That's finally why I did not let go of that faith. And that's finally why that faith did not let go of me.

Chapter 39: "Let the Peace of Christ Rule in Your Hearts" (Col. 3:15a NIV)

In one of the most beautiful passages in his letter to the Colossians, the Apostle wrote, "Let the peace of Christ rule in your hearts, since as members of one body you were called to peace. And be thankful."[1] All of us seek inner peace. Where can we discover such peace? It was Dante who once said, "In His will is our peace."[2] Outside God's will you will never find peace.[3] Whenever a believer loses that sense of inner peace, it might be their first clue that something in their life is off-center.[4]

Paul wrote, "Let the peace of Christ rule in your hearts..."[5] What does that mean? It sounded to me like some sort of mixed metaphor. I needed the Bible scholar, William Barclay, to straighten this out. He pointed out that the word Paul used for "rule" actually means "umpire" (or "referee"). To express this Bible verse differently means that you are allowing your inner feeling to be your umpire in any dilemma you're confronting.[6] In this way, when you literally feel "at peace" about a decision you are making, then you know you are in God's will and that this is the right decision. So may Christ's peace always be your referee.

A member of my church in Lancaster County, PA, was having breakfast with me one day. He was reflecting on this verse of scripture when he made this analogy. He said to me, "You know, when you go to a supermarket and stand right in front of the automatic door, it will open if you're standing in range of the sensor. But if you move to one side or the other, it's not going to open at all. That's just the way it is with our life in the Lord. That's why I think St. Paul said, "Let the peace of Christ rule in your hearts.""[7]

There's another insight that came to me. Perhaps it's a practical spin-off. When faced with a difficult decision, I've noticed that often the choice might be between an easy path or a difficult path. And most of the time (it seems to be a rule of thumb) the difficult path is ultimately going to be the correct one, the one that will bring you that serenity, that peace of Christ. For instance, let's imagine that you've hurt someone's feelings. You don't know whether to return to that person and apologize, or to go to the Lord and say you're sorry, thereby by-passing the one you had offended. If you go back to the one you had hurt, you'll have to "eat crow"; you'll have to endure your embarrassment. If you simply let it slide by conversing with the Lord, it's easier on your nervous system. But choosing the difficult path is generally the one that will bring you the peace of Christ. Then you will know that you are in God's will: QED.

A favorite proverb says, "Trust in the Lord with all your heart and lean not on your own understanding; in all your ways acknowledge him, and he will make your paths straight."[8] If you are reluctant to bring to the Lord your small decisions, you will probably defer bringing Him the larger ones. The prophet Isaiah wrote, "You will keep in perfect peace him whose mind is steadfast because he trusts in you."[9] St. Paul wrote, "Do not be anxious about anything, but in everything, by prayer and petition, with thanksgiving, present your requests to God. And the peace of God, which transcends all understanding, will guard your hearts and minds in Christ Jesus."[10]

In her powerful autobiography, The Hiding Place, Corrie ten Boom described a terrifying night, during the Second World War, when German and British planes were engaging in dogfights overhead. Corrie later wrote that, during those scary aerial duels one night, she lay in bed, when she happened to hear her sister downstairs. Betsie was puttering in the kitchen. Corrie ran downstairs to join her.

The two of them sat at the table, sipping tea and talking until the night sky was quiet. Then Corrie bade her sister good night and climbed back upstairs. Groping her way to her bed in the pitch black, she felt around for her pillow. Something hard and sharp was lying on it: a jagged slice of metal nearly a foot long! She called to her sister. Betsie stood there, aghast and kept saying "It was on your pillow, on your pillow."

Corrie understood what she was implying and with a sense of awe, replied, "Betsie, if I hadn't heard you in the kitchen..." But Betsie interrupted her. "Corrie, don't think about that. Don't focus on all the 'ifs'. In the Kingdom of God there aren't any 'ifs'. There's no place in our house or in the world that is safer than any other place. The only safe place is in God's will."[11]

"Let the peace of Christ rule in your hearts, since as member of one body you were called to peace."[12] We are called together to share God's peace with one another. We live in a society of "rugged individualism". Sometimes we get so caught up in being an individual and "doing our own thing" that we forget other people. Yet we are saved together, as a family of God. Paul added, "And be thankful."[13]

Years ago, a boat with many passengers was wrecked during a storm on Lake Michigan. Students from Northwestern University converged on the scene to team up to rescue those helpless, hapless passengers. One student, Edward Spencer, saved seventeen from the sinking ship. Years later, at a service in Los Angeles, an evangelist spoke about this incident that had occurred in Evanston, Illinois. And he mentioned the courageous young man who had managed to rescue so many.

Suddenly a man in the audience began to shout, "He's right here! Edward Spencer is present with us!" The startled evangelist invited him to the platform. An old white-haired man climbed slowly up the steps amidst an ovation. Dr. Torrey then asked him what he especially remembered about that night. He said, "I always remember this: not one of them ever thanked me."[14] Jesus went out on a limb for each of us. Never forget it. "And be thankful."[15]

Chapter 40: "With Gratitude" (Col. 3:16c NIV)

Catherine Marshall wrote about a friend of hers who had a happy marriage, a successful husband, health, wealth, and security. However, she had no spiritual life and subsequently experienced no inner peace. She felt empty inside. Catherine told her that, just as our bodies require physical food, our souls require spiritual food. The woman had neglected to feed her spirit.[1] Paul wrote, "Let the word of Christ dwell in you richly..."[2] Those Bible verses that I have intentionally - or sometimes unintentionally - memorized have come back to my mind just when I needed them. Long ago the psalmist wrote, "I have hidden your word in my heart that I might not sin against you."[3]

There was the terrible day when my dad died. The hospital nurses spent a long time "fixing him up" and then invited my mother and me to come into his hospital room. We walked in hushed silence, on tiptoe, as if we were stepping on holy ground. My mom stood beside the man she had been married to for over half a century. She began to speak aloud, and all that she said, over and over, was, "God is our refuge and strength; God is our refuge and strength." (Psalm 46:1 KJV). Her quoting those words is an example of hiding God's Word in our heart.

There is an ancient story about three horsemen who were traveling together when, out of nowhere, a stranger approached them. He told them, prophetically, that they would come upon a dry creek bed. There they would dismount, stoop down, and gather up as many stones as they wanted from the riverbed. However, they would wind up being happy and sad at the same time.

True to the stranger's prediction, they soon came to the riverbed and saw a field of stones scattered all about. Casually, they picked up some samples, put them into their pockets, and rode off. Later, when they examined their find, they discovered, to their amazement, that these nondescript stones had transformed into diamonds, sapphires, emeralds, and rubies. Then they recalled the stranger's warning that they would be happy and sad at the same time, they were happy for what they had, but sad that they hadn't filled up their saddlebags.[4]

That dried riverbed is like the Scripture. It's filled with maybe thousands of verses. They don't seem important to our life, but we stoop down and casually collect a few handfuls of them. Upon later examination in our life, we discover them to be precious promises. Then we kick ourselves, realizing that we could have retrieved more.[5] So, "Let the word of Christ dwell in you richly..."[6]

Paul added, "...as you teach and admonish one another with all wisdom, and as you sing psalms, hymns and spiritual songs with gratitude in your hearts to God."[7] We usually think of singing out loud, but if you happen to be a monotone like me, your witness will drive everyone else away in headlong flight, so I learn to sing silently, in my heart, to God. To the woman at the well, Jesus said, "Yet a time is coming and has now come when the true worshipers will worship the Father in spirit and in truth, for they are the kind of worshipers the Father seeks."[8] He doesn't read the score; He reads the heart.

A missionary was introducing a tourist to her mission church in Egypt. She was excited about his having the opportunity to hear the impassioned singing of men and women who had only recently come to the Lord. As they began to sing, the tourist became painfully aware of the fact that none of them had an ear for music. It was a cacophony of sounds. Still, when they were finished, the missionary turned and asked the tourist, "Wasn't that beautiful? (The question must have sounded like a sick joke.) But as a dedicated missionary, she had invested her whole life in leading men and women to Jesus. Their prayers and praise made celestial music in her heart.[9] For they sang the song of the redeemed.

Chapter 41: "Do All in the Name of Jesus" (Col. 3:17b NIV)

"And whatever you do, whether in word or deed, do it all in them of the Lord Jesus, giving thanks to God the Father through him."[1] In all of your labor, we are never to forget that sharing God's love through Christ Jesus must be our top priority. Christians tend to forget that and to put lesser concerns first. I have always deeply appreciated the following parable I was privileged to read.

Dr. S.D. Gordon, with his sanctified imagination, described a conversation in Heaven between the Archangel Gabriel and the Risen Christ after His ascension. Gabriel looked at Him with great concern and said, "Lord, it must have been excruciating for you down there, enduring persecution, rejection, desertion by your friends." Jesus said, "Gabriel, it still cuts deep and is too painful for me to talk about." Gabriel ventured to ask, "Do the people there on earth realize what you have done for them?" Jesus replied, "Only a small group understands so far."

Gabriel grew concerned. "But what is your plan to tell others and spread the word? How do you intend to tell the whole world that you died for them?" Jesus answered, "Oh, I asked Peter, James and John and some others to make it their number one priority." Gabriel, growing more skeptical, said, "But suppose they forget? Or suppose that, as time passes, they lose their energy, enthusiasm and motivation. Or suppose that their successors, two thousand years from now, simply get too busy and wrapped-up in doing things - maybe even good things - that they don't share the gospel with others? What other plan to you have?" And Jesus answered, "Gabriel, I have no other plans."[2]

Whatever you decide to say or do, do it all in the name of Jesus. I used to do everything in the name of Jerry Crossley. I did it so that others would surround me with applause. I liked that feeling of being affirmed, validated, appreciated, reassured. To what end? If people respond to me, they are guaranteed a friendship that lasts a lifetime (mine or theirs). If they respond to Jesus, they are guaranteed a friendship that will last for eternity. On the last night of His life, Jesus said, "Now this is eternal life: that they may know you, the only true God, and Jesus Christ whom you have sent."[3]

In my early thirties I was a member of a Christian motorcycle club known as "The Christian Wheels". Our expressed goal was to introduce people of every age, race, ethnicity, background, etc. to Jesus. We knew that our message had the potential to change lives. We used to hand out a little card whenever we had the privilege of helping someone out. The card said, "If you forget me, you've lost nothing. If you forget Jesus, you've lost everything."

"And whatever you do, whether in word or deed, do it all in the name of the Lord Jesus..."[4] His name has authority.[5] Remember the episode described in Acts chapter 4: The Temple guard arrested Peter and John because they viewed these followers of the Risen Christ as troublemakers. The next day the members of the Sanhedrin gathered together to give the apostles a hearing. They had healed a crippled beggar at the Temple gate. Their inquisitors "had Peter and John brought before them and began to question them: 'By what power or what name did you do this?' Then Peter, filled with the Holy spirit, said to them: 'Rulers and elders of the people! If we are being called to account today for an act of kindness shown to a cripple and are asked how he was healed, then know this, you and all the people of Israel: It is by the name of Jesus Christ of Nazareth, whom you crucified but whom God raised from the dead, that this man sits before you healed...Salvation is found in no one else, for there is no other name under heaven given to men by which we must be save.'"[6]

There is power in the name of Jesus. People all around us are accustomed to using His name profanely, but whenever they do, it cheapens it. I want to reserve His name for special occasions: for prayer and praise. I don't want to ever cheapen it by using it casually and unthinkingly. What was probably an early Christian hymn was quoted by Paul in his pastoral letter to the Christians in Philippi. It says, "Therefore God exalted him to the highest place and gave him the name that is above every name, that at the name of Jesus every knee should bow, in heaven and on earth, and under the earth, and every tongue confess that Jesus Christ is Lord, to the glory of God the Father."[7]

"And whatever you do, whether in word or deed, do it all in the name of the Lord Jesus, giving thanks to God the Father through him."[8] One Sunday afternoon, March 13th, 1994, our church in Lancaster County, Pennsylvania celebrated a Spring Concert. We were privileged to have with us the New Holland Band, presenting a beautiful and memorable three-hour concert in memory of some very special people who had passed away the previous year.

Just before they played "The Holy City", Mr. Marlin Houck, band director, prefaced the performance by saying something like this: "Mr. Paul Russell died this past year. He was always a very dedicated and strong supporter of the New Holland Band. He sang many bass solos in his church choir and once told me that his favorite was "The Holy City". He loved it. Therefore, it is with distinct pleasure that the band presents this selection to you in his name." Think about that. Because of Paul Russell and the influence of his guiding spirit, the band was going to share this special selection with the whole community, in his name.

Because of Jesus and the influence of His guiding Spirit, we are going to present to our community everything we say and everything we do, all in the matchless name of Jesus, "giving thanks to God the Father through him."

Chapter 42: "Wives...Husbands" (Col. 3:18-19 NIV)

In the pastoral letter that the Colossians had received these words resounded, "And whatever you do, whether in word or deed, do it all in the name of the Lord Jesus, giving thanks to God the Father through him"[1] These words weren't intended to be an abstract theological concept. They were meant to have practical application to every relationship we have: our marriages, our parenthood, our jobs, everything. Our first missions field is our own home. The Lord cares very much how we live out our faith in our home.[2] There's a little plaque which hung in my grandmother's dining room. It said, "Christ is the Head of this house,/ The Unseen Guest at every meal,/ The Silent Listener to every conversation."

So Paul wrote the ensuing verses: "Wives, submit to your husbands, as is fitting in the Lord."[3] In America's egalitarian society, emphasizing equality between men and women, this verse becomes a challenge. Bear with me, and with Paul, and let's see if we can detect the Divine principles behind these verses. Why is it that the Apostle addresses the woman first? Is he just trying to be polite? No, he addresses the wife first because she is most often the glue that holds the whole family together.[4]

That's certainly true in my own family. My mother was the center of our family life. Now my wife is the center. She is the magnet to whom each family member inevitably gravitates. She's like the sun, around which our family orbits. So Paul addresses the wives first. He says, "Wives, submit." In the world of Paul's day, women had very little social status anywhere. In Judaism, a wife was a possession, easily divorced by a discontented husband. In Hellenistic Society, she appears to be just an ornament, confined to her home, while her husband was free to pursue extra-curricular activities. So in both Jewish and Gentile societies, in the New Testament era, all the privileges belonged to the man, while all the obligations seemed to belong to the woman. Paul's approach to marriage was revolutionary.[5] He was advocating a reciprocity.[6]

At the beginning of the Bible we find the story of Adam and Eve. It can be read and appreciated either literally or metaphorically. Incidentally, there are a lot a Adam and Eve jokes. My favorite is this: one day Adam looked at Eve and asked, "Why did God make you so beautiful?" She said, "So you would love me, Adam." Adam thought about it and nodded his head in agreement. Then he asked, "But why did God make you so dumb?" Eve answered, "So I would love you."

"So the Lord God caused the man to fall into a deep sleep, and while he was sleeping, [God] took one of the man's ribs and closed up the place with flesh. Then the Lord God made a woman from the rib he had taken out of the man..."[7] I am now attempting to paraphrase the insight of Matthew Henry who wrote that the Lord did not make Eve out of Adam's head, to dominate him. He did not make Eve out of Adam's foot, to be beneath him and walked on. Instead, the Lord made her out of Adam's rib, to be continually by his side, his equal. He made her beneath his arm, to be protected. He made her from Adam's rib so that she would always be close to his heart.[8]

Now Paul turns to the men: "Husbands, love your wives, and do not be harsh with them."[9] Whenever a couple "falls in love" they imagine that it's easy to love each other. They are already consumed with romantic love, enjoying a wondrous chemistry that sparks and fizzes and gives new meaning to "getting fizzical". But when the romantic feelings fizzle out, they are either plunged into disillusionment or else discover a deeper, stronger love, an agape love, a selfless love.

There are lessons for all of us to learn along the way. Love your wife, not for yourself but for herself. With the help of the Holy Spirit love unconditionally with no strings attached. That means that you must respect the fact the she is a different person than you, and honor her uniqueness. The "M.C." of a TV show was interviewing a newlywed. He said, "Now you two have become one." She grimaced. Noting that he said, "Did it upset you when I said that you had become one?" "No." she answered. "What bothers me is...which one?" We are to love one another as Jesus loves each of us.

Sometimes men narcissistically get upset when they imagine that they are not getting all the love that they deserve. They feel cheated, rejected. How can we fix that? By fixing the wife? No. By fixing the husband! Instead of his obsessing over how much he's getting, he must begin focusing on how much he's giving. Above all, allow the Lord to love other persons through you. You'll be blessed when you become a channel of His love, His grace, His peace touching the life of someone else. Like your wife, for instance.

Remember that our Lord, when He was hanging on that cross, stretched between Heaven and earth, saw His own mother and His disciple John at the foot of the cross. They were grief-stricken. His heart went out to both of them. With deep compassion He whispered, "Dear woman, here is your son." He indicated that John should be her "new" son. Then He said, "John, here is your new mother."[10] Thus, He gave them into each other's keeping. So I picture Jesus saying now, daughter, here is your husband. Son, here is your wife. Love one another with My love.

Chapter 43: "Children...Fathers" (Col. 3:20-21 NIV)

The task of parenthood is really tough. It goes beyond being a sperm-donor or an egg-bearer. There are constant challenges that confront us. Fortunately for you, I've managed to compile a little list of instructions that will assist you in becoming a stupid parent. First, begin, in your child's infancy, to give him everything he wants. In this delightful way, your child will approach adulthood believing that everybody owes him a good living. Secondly, try never to be available to your child or else he'll always be coming to you to talk things over.

Thirdly, try disciplining your child only when you lose your temper. Then feel free to erupt like a volcano. The end-result of your performance will be that, someday, your child will have been enabled to pass all that violence to somebody else. Fourthly, if ever your child messes up, never let him forget it. Keep hounding him with his mistake. That way he'll be able to despise you. Fifthly, to help your child's sense of competition, persist in comparing him with someone else. "Why can't you be more like Jimmy or Sarah?" In that way, he can loathe both them and you.

Sixthly, instead of trying to give your child love, just hand him money as a substitute. Soon, he's not going to be looking for you at all. He's just going to be looking for your money. "Show me the money." Seventhly, pick up all the messes he makes. Then, as he grows up, he'll count on others to clean up after him. Eighth (is there an "eighthly"?) emphatically disagree with your spouse on how to raise your mutual child. That will spare your child the feeling of shock when your family is broken apart. Ninthly, don't bother raising your child in a community of faith. Be completely neutral. Wait until he's 21 and can make his own decision.[1]

We need God's wisdom to raise our children. So Paul wrote, "Children, obey your parents in everything, for this pleases the Lord."[2] See? This is not an option for your kids; it's not multiple choice. It is a duty not solely to the parents, but also to God. It is clearly written in the Bible, "Honor your father and your mother, so that you may live long in the land the Lord your God is giving you."[3]

That happens to be in the Ten Commandments, so don't go telling me, "Well, it's not written in stone," because it is.

Then Paul added fathers. "Fathers, do not embitter your children, or they will become discouraged."[4] One day I was talking to Rev. Frank Kensil, pastor of a Rescue Mission in North Philadelphia. He knew all about life in the ghetto. He was sharing with me his difficulty in communicating the Gospel. "Look, you attempt to say, 'God is a loving Father.' And that basic statement of the Christian faith makes no sense to them. They say in response, 'What's "love"? What's a "father"?' And your entire analogy collapses because they never had a loving father."

St. Paul admonished his new Christians to avoid embittering their children. Today we'd probably caution, "Don't keep putting them down." I once saw a Wayside Pulpit which announced, "Children need models, not critics." In my own life I don't remember all the people who put me down, for they were a multitude. Often they were members of the churches I served. I remember only those few who picked me up, who cared, who took the time to encourage me.

"They will become discouraged." John Newton did. He once wrote this sad disclosure. He said that he knew that his father loved him, but his father didn't want to show it. The result of the father's reticence to express his love openly is that the child's spirit is broken.[5] Deprived of that, the child will grow up feeling unloved and unlovable, and this fundamental sadness will be hard to shake.

A young woman named Angie grew up with a distorted self-image. Ever since she was a little girl she found that she could never earn her father's acceptance. In spite of all her efforts, she felt rejected. She worked hard to earn his love, but it didn't happen. At school she created artwork that she couldn't wait to show her daddy, but he always found fault with what she had made. Even when she got all dressed up for church, he'd criticize how she looked. She was a few pounds overweight, and he berated her for that.

All these deceitful lies about herself she believed because her father, her authority figure, had told her so. She grew up feeling like a loser, believing that she was ugly from the inside-out. Angie was convinced that no one could ever love her, that she was destined to remain unlikable. Then one day a friend invited her to church. She listened to the Gospel and invited Jesus into her heart. Instead of seeing herself through the eyes of her earthly father, she began to see herself through the eyes of her Heavenly Father. She saw a child of God, loved and forever cherished.[6]

Chapter 44: "It is the Lord Christ You are Serving" (Col. 3:24b NIV)

The new Testament attitude to slavery, all-pervasive in the Roman world, is a puzzlement. What are we to make of the Christian response. In his letter to the new Christians in Colossae, Paul wrote, "Slaves, obey your earthly masters in everything; and do it, not only when their eye is on you and to win their favor, but with sincerity of heart and reverence for the Lord."[1]

So here is how I approach it. Instead of looking at "slaves" and "masters", let's make a quick translation and reconsider the passage in terms of "worker" and "employer". Then let's see if we can identify the important biblical principle underlying the verse. The culture, the economies, the geo-politics may change, but the biblical principle remains the same.

There are many Christians who are willing to live their faith and "walk the walk" if they are in a Christian setting. In other words, at church or Sunday School they will be exemplars of the Gospel. But in a secular setting they'll drop their act. Yet a genuine Christian will want to consistently live out their faith, even if unobserved. In my understanding, integrity means wholeness of character. What we believe and how we behave must be of one piece.

A church nominating committee met to choose men and women for church offices. In the course of making their choices, they happened to nominate someone who proved to be controversial. One member of the committee cautioned the others not to nominate this particular man for an office in the congregation. "He allows his surroundings to shape the way he behaves. For instance, if he's around fellow believers, he will pose as a deeply spiritual person. When around nonbelievers, he is very profane. He's not a very good ambassador for Christ."[2]

"Whatever you do, work at it with all your heart, as working for the Lord, not for men..."[3] With all your heart! Whatever you do! On Arturo Toscvanini's 80th birthday, reporters asked his son what his father considered his greatest achievement. He answered that his father never thought about his accomplishments in those terms. Instead, he tended to see each task he was endeavoring to do at the moment - whether directing a symphony orchestra or peeling an orange - as the biggest endeavor of his life.[4] And that's just the way it should be with you. Whatever you do, do it wholeheartedly. Why?

"Work at it with all your heart, as working for the Lord..."[5] That's why. How quickly and easily we forget that we are working for Christ. Once a passerby happened to observe two stonemasons working to cut a stone. He stopped and asked the first man just what he was doing. The worker gave an abrupt answer. "What does it look like? I'm cutting a stone!" The passerby approached the second stonemason with the same question. The man looked up and said, with a sense of pride, "Sir, I happen to be building a cathedral!" The first worker saw his labor as only a job. The other saw something holy about his effort.[6]

Above all the cacophony and confusion of life, we hear Jesus' words, "Verily I say unto you, inasmuch as ye have done it unto one of the least of these my brethren, ye have done it unto me." (Matt. 25:40 KJV). In his book, You Are Loved and Forgiven, Lloyd John Ogilvie recounted the following episode: Many years earlier he had an associate who worked with a greater intensity and dedication than any other clergy Ogilvie knew. Tirelessly he labored to perform every task assigned or suggested to him. He went beyond the call of duty. One day Dr. Ogilvie thanked him for all his hard work. His associate smiled quietly, then said, "I'm glad you're pleased, but actually I'm not doing it for you; I'm doing it for Him." Ogilvie concluded that the Apostle Paul would have appreciated his answer.[7]

"...you know that you will receive an inheritance from the Lord as a reward. It is the Lord Christ you are serving."[8] One day a shop owner had to leave on business, and he left his young employee to mind the store. In the meantime a con-artist entered and tried to sell him a bad bill of goods. He was a smooth, fast-talking wheeler dealer, yet he found the store employee resistant to his sales pitch. When he sensed that the young man was dragging his feet, he said, "Hey! It's alright. Remember, the master's not here." The young man pointed up and answered, "My Master is always here!" No matter what we say or do, our Master is always here. And you and I labor beneath His watchful eye.[9]

Chapter 45: "You Have a Master in Heaven" (Col. 4:1 NIV)

If you're like me, reading the daily newspaper or listening otherwise to the local news can become maddening. One reads about heinous crimes punished by light sentences or, sometimes, none. People can literally get away with murder. But remember that there's another Tribunal with the same insight. Paul wrote, "Anyone who does wrong will be repaid for his wrong, and there is no favoritism."[1] It's an equal-opportunity tribunal.

We read in Romans, "For we will all stand before God's judgment seat."[2] And in Galatians, "Do not be deceived: God cannot be mocked. A man reaps what he sows. The one who sows the please his sinful nature, from that nature will one who sows to please his sinful nature, from that nature will reap destruction; the one who sows to please the Spirit, from the Spirit will reap eternal life."[3] We have this little expression, "Whatever goes around comes around." That sounds biblical.

So don't waste your time judging others, because they have another Judge. "God didn't die and leave you 'boss'." In Romans we read, "Do not repay anyone evil for evil. Be careful to do what is right in the eyes of everybody. If it is possible, as far as it depends on you, live at peace with everyone. Do not take revenge, my friends, but leave room for God's wrath, for it is written, 'It is mine to avenge; I will repay.' says the Lord. On the contrary: 'If your enemy is hungry, feed him. If he is thirsty, give him something to drink. In doing this, you will heap burning coals on his head.' Do not be overcome by evil, but overcome evil with good."[4] Each of us is accountable.

We reap what we sow. There's a wonderful story that is even more wonderful because it's a true story. One night, amidst a terrible storm, a husband and wife crept into the lobby of a small hotel and begged the clerk for a room. With embarrassment he explained that, because there were three conventions in town, the little hotel was already filled to capacity, and there was absolutely nothing available. Then he cautiously added, "But I have my room here at the hotel, and because I'm here at the desk till tomorrow, it's unoccupied. I can't just turn you two out into the storm. Why don't you take my room?" The couple hesitated, but there was really nowhere else to go. So they took it. The next morning, as they check out, the customer spoke to the kind clerk who was still on duty, saying "You're just the kind of person who should be the manager of the best and biggest hotel in America. Someday I'm going to build it for you."

A couple of years later, the hotel clerk received a mysterious letter from the same man to whom he had given his own room one stormy night. In the letter was a personal invitation to come to New York City. The letter enclosed a round-trip ticket. When he arrived, his host escorted him to 5th Avenue and 34th Street, where a spectacular new building stood commandingly. "What is this building?" asked the clerk. The man said, "This is the hotel that I promised you. I just built it. You are to be the hotel manager." The clerk was stunned. "You're kidding me." "I assure you that I'm not." "Who are you?" My name is William Waldorf Astor." The name of the new manager was George C. Boldt. The name of the hotel was The Waldorf Astoria!"[5]

Those who do right will one day be rewarded. It's "in the Book". From the closing chapter of the closing book of the Bible comes this promise: "No longer will there be any curse. The throne of God and of the Lamb will be in the City, and his servants will serve him. Then you will see his face, and his name will be on their foreheads. There will be no more night. They will not need the light of a lamp or the light of the sun, for the Lord God will give them light. And they will reign forever and ever."[6]

The fourth chapter of Colossians begins with these problematic words, "Masters, provide your slaves with what is right and fair..."[7] Masters and slaves! Curiously, the man entrusted with the task of carrying this letter to the Colossians was himself a runaway slave named Onesimus. He had sought out Paul for refuge, and now Paul was sending him right back to his master, Philemon. So, of course, everyone probably wanted to hear what the Apostle had to say about slavery in general, or perhaps runaway slaves in particular.[8] Yet Paul did not attack the institution of slavery which was universally accepted across the Roman world.

In America we have seen our nation torn apart by the practice of human slavery. A terrible Civil War cost thousands of people their lives. But Paul was not forthcoming. I think that there are three reasons. First, slavery was woven into the fabric of the culture of Rome. It has been estimated that, in Paul's day, there were 60 million slaves. Had the Early Church opposed it openly, it would have been discredited. Paul did not oppose it head-on. Ralph Martin commented that Paul's letter was not a Magna Carta nor an Emancipation Proclamation.[9]

Secondly, the nature of the Gospel was not so much to reform social institutions as to transform human hearts.[10] Then, transformed hearts begin the task of reforming the social institutions and, thirdly, even though the slave was still a slave, if he or she was a Christian, then they were free in Christ.[11] The point that Paul was making is that slave masters must treat their slaves justly and fairly because their own Lord and Master cares very much about both masters and slaves.

That prompted Paul to write in his letter, "Masters, provide your slaves with what is right and fair, because you know that you also have a Master in heaven."[12] The life that is surrendered to Him is the freest life of all. J.T. Seamands hastens to remind us that we are not surrendering to a cruel autocrat, to a sadistic tyrant, but to a compassionate and loving Savior who wants the best for us.[13] In 1890 George Matheson wrote:

> Make me a captive, Lord,
> And then I shall be free.
> Force me to render up my sword,
> And I shall conqueror be.
> I sink in life's alarms
> When by myself I stand;
> Imprison me within Thine arms,
> And strong shall be my hand."[14]

Chapter 46: "Devote Yourselves to Prayer" (Col. 4:2 NIV)

It often happens, when we're talking with someone who is struggling with a problem, that we find ourselves asking, "Is there anything I can do for you?" When we ask this question, we usually are clueless about what we can or should do. One thing each of us can do is to pray for that person. I often respond, "I personally can't fix your problem, but I know Someone who can."

Paul wrote, "Devote yourselves to prayer, being watchful and thankful."[1] You'll never know how effective your prayer can be. The poet, Alfred Lord Tennyson, wrote, "More things are wrought by prayer / Than this world dreams of. / Wherefore, let thy voice / Rise like a fountain for me night and day."[2] William Carey was once criticized for all the time he was spending in prayer instead of his shoe store. He answered, "That's because my real business isn't shoes, it's prayer. Repairing customers' shoes is just a side job to help pay my bills." The Lord saw and honored His faithful follower. William Carey became a famous missionary in the Far East.[3] So I guess this man of prayer was finally more focused on souls than soles. Like William Carey - no matter what we do for a living - we should make prayer the business of our life.

"At Caesarea there was a man named Cornelius, a centurion in what was known as the Italian Regiment. He and all his family were devout and God - fearing; he gave generously to those in need and prayed to God regularly. One day at about three in the afternoon he had a vision. He distinctly saw an angel of God, who came to him and said, 'Cornelius!' Cornelius stared at him in fear. 'What is it, Lord?' he asked. The angel answered, 'Your prayers and gifts to the poor have come up as a memorial offering before God.'"[4]

Did you get that? Cornelius' many prayers were something more than wasted breath. They were a "memorial" before God. The Lord considered them something precious. So are your prayers. There are those heavy moments in our life when we feel that nobody is listening. William Barclay observed that even the most spiritual among us experience those terrible times when it seems that our prayers don't get past the ceiling. What should we do then? Keep on praying.[5]

Keep on praying, "being watchful and thankful."[6] The answer to prayer might come in a way we don't recognize and would least expect. So keep alert for the answer. A good friend of ours, Helen, shared with my wife and me a story about her mother. She was a very "earthy" woman who lived a worldly life and had no interest in anything spiritual. Her daughter constantly prayed for her: thirty years of unanswered prayers. Helen grew increasingly frustrated.

Then, one Sunday morning, as Helen was sitting in our little church in Northeast Philadelphia, her mother walked down the aisle and sat down beside her. It was her mother's first church visit in years. At the end of my sermon I felt led to give an "altar call", inviting congregants to come forward and kneel at the altar in prayer. Helen herself came forward and devoutly knelt at the altar, in prayer - once again - for her mother. When she opened her eyes, she saw her mother kneeling right beside her in prayer, seeking new life in Christ.

Helen later recounted that she was completely shocked. "I looked at her and saw her kneeling in prayer right beside me. In utter disbelief I said, 'Mother, what are you doing here?' Imagine that! I had been praying for the salvation of her soul for thirty years, and here I was, asking 'What are you doing here?'" God's timing is different than ours. So "devote yourselves to prayer, being watchful and thankful."[7]

Thankful that we have a loving Father God who treasures each of us and cherishes our prayers.

Chapter 47: "The Mystery of Christ" (Col. 4:3 NIV)

A good marriage really depends on good communication. That's what it takes to build trust. Over and over, in marriage counseling, distraught women have said, "My husband doesn't communicate with me at all. He doesn't listen to my feelings, and he doesn't share his own. I think that all of our problems stem from his reluctance, or inability to communicate." That's the way it is with us and our Father in Heaven. It's hard to maintain a relationship when you no longer communicate. And how do we communicate? Through prayer. We share our feelings and then listen.

Paul wrote, "Devote yourselves to prayer, being watchful and thankful. And pray for us, too..."[1] He cherished their prayers for his ministry, as every missionary does. After years of pastoral ministry, I have concluded that the Lord wants us to name names and be specific in our prayers. Warren Wiersbe speculated that our nice-sounding prayers, with their generalizations, don't demonstrate faith but ironically, our lack of faith. We're afraid of getting too specific with the Lord, so instead of getting to the point, we pussyfoot all around it.[2]

In one of the congregations I pastored in Philadelphia we were preparing for a weekend Lay Witness Mission. On such an occasion, maybe 20 to 40 lay people - representing many denominations - converge on your church and just candidly share their faith, their triumphs and defeats, etc. We find that the Holy Spirit is present with us. In preparation for this event I had inadvertently overlooked our shut-ins. When someone pointed out my oversight, I insensitively said, "Well, what can they do?" See, I was so accustomed to ministering to them that I never imaged what they could do to minister to us.

"What can they do," I casually said. A young woman softly and kindly answered, "Jerry, they can pray for us." The answer was so obvious. So we organized them to uphold us in prayer throughout our special weekend. They were thrilled to have been asked, and to have been included. They became our prayer warriors. The result was that miracles began to take place in our congregation, because men and women were engaged in prayer. The Lord had honored their faith.

Paul wanted prayer specifically "that God may open a door for our message..."[3] My mother frequently utilized the symbol of a door. She'd say to me, "Jerry, if you walk with the Lord, always remember that wherever one door closes, another will open. And God will lead you through the open door." Many a time you look ahead and see only a blank wall, a "no exit". But God can make a door where there is no door. Now what the Apostle was praying for was that this same God would open the door for the proclamation of His Word.

After one of their missionary journeys, Paul and Barnabas sailed back to their headquarters in Antioch. "On arriving there, they gathered the church together and reported all that God had done through them and how He had opened the door of faith to the Gentiles."[4] Again, to the Corinthians, Paul wrote, "Now when I went to Troas to preach the gospel of Christ [I] found that the Lord had opened a door..."[5] And in the closing book of the Bible we read, "See, I have placed before you an open door that no one can shut."[6]

Pray "so that we may proclaim the mystery of Christ, for which I am in chains."[7] What is this mystery of Christ? Now an open secret, it is the revelation that God loves Jews and Gentiles alike.[8] One day the author of the Gospel according to St. John would write the immortal words, "For God so loved the world that he have his one and only Son, that whoever believes in him shall not perish but have eternal life."[9] Jesus' arms spread wide enough to include everyone. To the Galatians Paul wrote, "There is neither Jew nor Greek, slave nor free, male nor female, for you are all one in Christ Jesus."[10]

A man named Dean Hatfield has had the wonderful privilege of leading hundreds of men and women to the Lord. However, he once went through a time of spiritual drought when he failed to lead anyone anywhere. So he prayed fervently, "Dear Lord, open my heart to anyone who needs You. Then open the door so that I can bring them into Your presence." Not long after making this prayer, his phone range. Wrong number! Disgusted, the caller hung up.

The phone rang again. Again, the wrong number. Same caller, who could not believe that twice he had called the wrong number. He was about to hang up when Dean Hatfield urged him not to. After all, maybe the phone caller's disappointment was actually God's appointment. Maybe he was supposed to call this "wrong" number. Unsure of this line of reasoning, the caller held onto the phone and just listened. Dean led him to Christ. Within the ensuring year, his life was transformed. He led friends and family to the Lord. Today he's a full-time pastor. All because of a wrong number. All because of a prayer.

Chapter 48: "Make the Most of Every Opportunity" (Col. 4:5b NIV)

As I was growing up, I always wanted to be in the "in" group and never be considered an "outsider". However, being a rather diminutive boy with a high-pitched voice, I was always consigned to the role of an outsider. As a consequence. I have always identified with those outsiders. I can appreciate Paul's admonition, "Be wise in the way you act toward outsiders..."[1]

In his commentary, Martin Franzmann wrote that to care about outsiders is to recognize that Jesus went to the cross for outsiders, shed His blood for outsiders, and lives again for outsiders. Finally, it is to realize that, for Jesus, there are no "outsiders", that all of us are invited into the Father's house.[2] To the Ephesians Paul wrote, "...remember that at that time you were separate from Christ, excluded from citizenship in Israel and foreigners to the covenants of the promise, without hope and without God in the world. But now in Christ Jesus you who once were far away have been brought near through the blood of Christ."[3]

We follow a faith that makes exclusive demands but is always inclusive in its outreach "You yourselves are our letter, written on our hearts, known and read by everybody...written not with ink but with the Spirit of the living God, not on tablets of stone but on tablets of human hearts."[4] So we are the Lord's postcard to the lost, saying, "Miss you. Wish you were here." What is the best way we can conduct ourselves wisely toward the outsider? I think we do this simply by allowing Him to love others through us.

Paul enjoins us to "make the most of every opportunity."[5] Just as some people frequent flea markets and yard sales, we should be looking for opportunities to speak a good word for Jesus.[6] Even in my pastoral ministry, where I was paid to be a professional witness, I often deliberately by-passed opportunities to share my faith. Why? Sometimes it was just fear of rejection. The other person might turn me down for intruding upon their privacy. Then the moment passed by, and the opportunity was gone. I was left with regret.

"Let your conversation be always full of grace, seasoned with salt, so that you may know how to answer everyone."[7] Often I was so interested in expounding my own agenda that I paid no attention to the other person's thought and feelings. I constantly have to re-learn the lesson that I must focus on them. I must spend more time listening than speaking. And never engage in theological arguments. They serve only to make the person you're addressing more defensive. In 2 Timothy we read this instruction: "Don't have anything to do with foolish and stupid arguments, because you know they produce quarrels. And the Lord's servant must not quarrel; instead, he must be kind to everyone..."[8] Remember, you can never argue a person into the Kingdom of God.

One night an atheist was addressing his audience when he threw down a challenge to everyone there in the lecture hall. "I invite anyone who thinks he can disprove my arguments to come up to this platform." For a few moments everyone just sat there, stone silent. Then an old man rose from his seat and came up to the platform. "Alright. Prove to me that I'm wrong," snarled the speaker. Wordlessly, the elderly man removed an orange from his pocket, peeled it, and nonchalantly ate it in front of the atheist. "So where's your proof?" "Well" answered the challenger, "How did my orange taste?"

"How should I know? I never tasted it" "That's right", the old man said. "I just wanted to show you how I became a believer. I tasted it, and it was good."[9]

One of my most favorite psalms is the 34th: "I sought the Lord, and he answered me; he delivered one from all my fears. Those who look to him are radiant; their faces are never covered with shame. This poor man called, and the Lord heard him; he saved him out of all his trouble. The angel of the Lord encamps around those who fear him, and he delivers them. Taste and see that the Lord is good; blessed [are they] who take refuge in him."[10]

In matters of faith, no one else can taste for you; you have to do your own tasting!

Chapter 49: "Fellow Servant" (Col. 4:7 NIV)

Towards the conclusion of his letter to the Colossians, the Apostle Paul becomes a name-dropper. "Tychicus will tell you all of the news about me."[1] He was the one who helped carry the offering for the poor all the way to Jerusalem (Acts 20:4). Furthermore, he carried Paul's letter to the Ephesians (Eph. 6:21, 2 Tim. 4:12). So here is a man who was Paul's personal messenger.[2] Maybe you would not consider him a "hero of the faith". He just carried the mail [which today is part of our New Testament] and completed the tasks that Paul gave him. He performed a humble service in Jesus' name.[3] Sometimes we are happy to serve the Lord in a big way, but not in a small way. In the splashy, dramatic way we can sort of showcase ourselves. But perhaps no one will take notice of our menial tasks - except Jesus.

Paul must have loved this man because he paid him the supreme compliment, "He is a dear brother, a faithful minister and fellow servant in the Lord."[4] "A faithful minister"! Elsewhere Paul wrote, "Now it is required that those who have been given a trust must prove faithful."[5] The Lord isn't summoning us to be rich or prominent or successful or famous: just faithful. I am friends with a devout Methodist pastor of a growing congregation. He just received terrifying news from his urologist. Bill has an extremely rare tumor that is inoperable and fatal. His lifespan is less than six months. As he cried out to God, he heard Him say, "Stop looking at dates on the calendar. Trust me and continue to pastor your people." Rev. Bill asked, "Lord, what do you want from me?" And He said, "Just be faithful."

When I was in eighth grade, graduating from James Russell Lowell Elementary School in Philadelphia, there was a very special awards ceremony. The greatest and most coveted award awarded to the highest-achieving student, was the American Legion Award. I fantasized hearing the school principal intone, "And now the award presented to the most brilliant student in the graduating class, the American Legion medal, is presented to Jerry Crossley." He didn't call my name. Instead, the cherished award was presented - justifiably, I hasten to add - to Barry Bloom.

Then came the Forefathers Award. I think it was presented to the most promising student. I strained forward to hear my name. It would make my parents so proud. But the principal said, "William Rummler" - again a decent choice. Then came the P.T.A. award. This time my name was called. "To Jerry Crossley, awarded by the Parent Teachers Association for "Dependability". Faithfulness! In retrospect, maybe the PT.A. award was the best one of all. Maybe, in the long-run, it's better to be dependable than to be brilliant. And here's another angle: we cannot choose to be brilliant, but we can choose to be dependable.

"Tychicus...is a dear brother, a faithful minister and fellow servant in the Lord."[6] We should glory not in being lords but in being servants. Dwight L. Moody stated that the real measure of a person is not how many people wait on him, but on how many people he waits on.[7] Paul's beloved brother Tychicus carried three letters from Paul. He carried Colossians, Ephesians, and Philemon. That's a big chunk of the Bible.[8] We may never know how important our service was until we get to Heaven.[9]

Paul wrote, "I am sending him to you for the express purpose that you may know about our circumstances and that he may encourage your hearts".[10] What a joy it is to be an encourager. After having lived 88 years in this world, I have concluded that humanity is divided into two kinds of people: lifter-uppers and putter-downers, between encouragers and discouragers. Unfortunately, it's not evenly divided. Even in churches, unbelievably, there are more putter-downers than lifter-uppers. Tychicus was being sent to encourage the followers of Christ Jesus. Maybe you and I are being sent on the same mission.

One of the hymns I love is this:

"O Master, let me walk with thee
In lowly paths of service free;
Tell me thy secret;
Help me bear
The strain of toil, the fret of care.

"Help me the slow of heart to move

By some clear, winning word of love;
Teach me the wayward
Feet to stay,
And guide them in the homeward way.

"In hope that sends a shining ray
Far down the future's broadening way,
In peace that only
Thou canst give,
With thee, O Master, let me live."[11]

Chapter 50: "Onesimus" (Col. 4:9 NIV)

Paul was introducing all his helpers to the Christians of Colossae. He noted Tychicus, and then added, "He is coming with Onesimus, our faithful and dear brother, who is one of you."[1] Everyone in town know Onesimus or know about him. He was a fugitive, a runaway slave, who had fled his master, Philemon. Philemon was a member of the congregation. Onesimus could legally be captured and executed, but he ran to the Apostle who was a prisoner in Rome. He took refuge with Paul who led him into a brand-new faith. It's possible - says R. Kent Hughes - that Onesimus' original intention was to lose himself in the large slave population. He could hide from his owner, but he could not camouflage himself from the eye of God.[2]

Now Paul was sending him back to his Master and included, along with his letter to the church, a personal note to Philemon, the slave-owner. In it, Paul played all the aces he was holding in his hand. He expressed his desire that Philemon take his slave back not so much as a slave, but as a brother in the Lord. "I appeal to you for my son Onesimus, who became my son while I was in chains. Formerly he was useless to you, but now he has become useful both to you and to me. I am sending him - who is my very heart - back to you."[3]

Paul felt duty-bound to send the fugitive slave back to the slaveholder. This would involve extreme risk because the slave owner had absolute authority over a slave who was considered just a disposable piece of property, not even human. He could beat, torture, and kill him with impunity. For instance, one poor slave who accidentally over-heated his master's bath water was thrown into an oven and roasted alive.[4] A runaway slave invited the most extreme punishment: crucifixion. So Paul was sending back Onesimus with fear and trembling.[5]

Paul was pleading for a reconciliation. "Perhaps the reason he was separated from you for a little while was that you might have him back for good - no longer as a slave, but better than a slave, as a dear brother. He is very dear to me but even dearer to you, both as a man and as a brother in the Lord."[6] In retrospect, it's clear that Paul wasn't sending him back to an old relationship. Instead, he was sending him forward into a new relationship that would reflect the grace of God. Elsewhere Paul had written, "Therefore, if anyone is in Christ, he is a new creation; the old has gone, the new has come!"[7]

To sweeten the deal, he added, "If he has done you any wrong or owes you anything, charge it to me. I, Paul, am writing this with my own hand. I will pay it back..."[8] It's entirely possible that this runaway slave had not fled empty-handed. He had perhaps helped himself to a little fast cash.[9] Generously, Paul offered to pay any outstanding charges in the same way that the Good Samaritan offered to pay the innkeeper for any charges incurred.[10]

Paul had the distinct privilege of leading both men - the slave and his master - to the Lord. That's plainly why he could write to Philemon, "...not to mention that you owe me your very self...Confident of your obedience, I write to you, knowing that you will do even more than I ask."[11] Well, what finally happened? At the end of the first century a man named Onesimus became bishop of the church at Ephesus.[12] Would that not be a surprise ending? Would that not be so like the Lord?

Paul wrote to Philemon that "Onesimus...is one of you."[13] It's our human propensity to seek out like-minded friends and allies as "we" and the other people, the aliens, as "they". We have an "us-them" mentality. Mindful of this, Paul said, in effect, "I want you to see Onesimus not as a fugitive slave but as one of you: a faithful and beloved brother.

Tychicus and Onesimus "will tell you everything that is happening here."[14] In other words, whenever we followers of Jesus hear about all the miraculous events that are transpiring, whenever we see His power dramatically and convincingly demonstrated, our faith will be quickened; our souls inspired.[15] These two men were bearing pastoral letters that would be preserved. Little did they know that, two thousand years later, people would still be reading them long after the great cities of the Roman Empire were rubble and rubbish.[16]

The prophet Isaiah wrote, "The grass withers and the flowers fall, but the word of our God stands forever."[17]

Chapter 51: "Welcome Him" (Col. 4:10c NIV)

Paul introduces more co-workers to the Colossians: "My fellow prisoner Aristarchus sends you his greetings..."[1] He had proven himself to be a loyal friend to his mentor, staying by his side through many dangerous situations and accompanying him to imprisonment in Rome. He shared Paul's confinement.[2] A Hellenistic (Greek-speaking) Jew who had become a Christian.[3] Aristarchus was willing to take a stand for what he believed, even to the point of being arrested and thrown into prison.[4]

He didn't just go to prison; he went to prison for a cause. He went because of his loyalty to the Gospel. In our society today, people's practice of religion seems to be determined by convenience. "I'll make sacrifices so long as it's convenient." When was making a sacrifice ever "convenient"? In the 19th century Henry Thoreau chose to go to jail rather than pay his taxes to a state that openly endorsed human slavery. His literary friend, Ralph Waldo Emerson, came to see him and asked, "Why Henry, what are you doing in here?" Thoreau replied, "Why Ralph, what are you doing out there?"[5]

"My fellow prisoner Aristarchus sends you his greetings, as does Mark, the cousin of Barnabas."[6] The very first time we hear about Mark is near the end of his gospel where it tells about Jesus' arrest in the Garden. Then comes this cryptic passage: "A young man, wearing nothing but a linen garment, was following Jesus. When they seized him, he fled naked, leaving his garment behind."[7] Who was this mysterious person? Possibly Mark himself (he wasn't naming names). He was probably writing about himself in the third person.[8]

Perhaps this man was a person who would readily choose flight over fight. If so, I can certainly identify with him. I know what it feels like to consciously let Jesus down, to turn tail and run away. Paul and Barnabas took him with them on their first missionary journey.[9] Then come those enigmatic words, "From Paphos, Paul and his companions sailed to Perga in Pamphylia, where John [Mark] left them to return to Jerusalem."[10] It was an unscheduled departure, and Paul was angry. Why did John Mark leave them?

What had transpired to make this young man, once again, turn tail and run away?

Honestly, nobody knows. We can hazard some guesses. Maybe he had second thoughts as he contemplated the rigors of a missionary journey. (He couldn't stand the heat, so he got out of the kitchen.) Maybe he was just plain home-sick, suffering separation anxiety. Or perhaps he left because he could not stand to watch his beloved cousin Barnabas gradually take a back seat to the more aggressive Paul. Or maybe he left because, as a Jewish Christian, he really disagreed with the policy of admitting Gentiles, wholesale, into their fellowship. But, for whichever reason or combination of reasons, he left.[11] And it left a bad taste in Paul's mouth. R. Kent Hughes commented that Paul wasn't in the business of operating a travel agency, and he wasn't looking to include any cowardly tourists on his team.[12]

In a passage recorded by Luke in Acts 15, we read this: "Sometime later Paul said to Barnabas, 'Let us go back and visit the brothers in all the towns where we preached the word of the Lord and see how they are doing.' Barnabas wanted to take John, also called Mark, with them, but Paul did not think it wise to take him, because he had deserted them in Pamphylia and had not continued with them in the work. They had such a sharp disagreement that they parted company."[13]

But sometime between that incident and Paul's letter to the Colossians a beautiful reconciliation had taken place. Paul could not have known it, but one day John Mark would sit down and write the first gospel, which would become known in the Church as "The Gospel according to Saint Mark". "Saint"!

So Paul would write in his pastoral letter, "My fellow prisoner Aristarchus sends you his greetings, as does Mark, the cousin of Barnabas. (You have received instructions about him; if he comes to you, welcome him.)[14] Why did he need to tell them that? Probably because the congregation knew all about John Mark's desertion. Just when the Apostle Paul needed him, he decided to go A.W.O.L.[15] Ironically, at the very end of his own ministry, Paul would write to

Timothy, "Get Mark and bring him with you, because he is helpful to me in my ministry."[16]

I bet that there are people you've written off, too. They hurt you deeply, and you are embittered. You have used all your powers of reason simply to rationalize your emotions. So you're done with that relationship and say, with more than a little self-righteousness, "I'll never have anything to do with that person again." You feel completely justified in your own eyes.

But not in God's eyes. He has commanded you to let go of the past and to reach out with healing and redemptive love. That's what He has given us. And he gave it to you, not to hug it to yourself as your own cherished possession, but to share it with someone else, someone with whom you've had an adversarial relationship. Once Jesus said, "Freely you have received; freely give."[17]

Chapter 52: "They Have Proved a Comfort to Me" (Col. 4:11b NIV)

It was more than just the Apostle Paul interested in the welfare of the Colossians; a whole lot of fellow Christians also wanted to send their love, prayers, and best wishes. Paul mentions some of them by name. "Jesus, who is called Justus, also sends greetings."[1] We know nothing about this man, a Jewish Christian, except his name.[2] He wasn't exactly a big star in the apostolic firmament.[3] But then, neither are we. God doesn't always use big stars. Many times He works through ordinary people.

So Paul expanded this thought in his first letter to the congregation in Corinth: "Brothers, think of what you were when you were called. Not many of you were wise by human standards; not many were influential; not many were of noble birth. But God chose the foolish things of the world to shame the wise; God chose the weak things of the world to shame the strong. He chose the lowly things of this world and the despised things - and the things that are not - to nullify the things that are, so that no one may boast before him."[4]

Then Paul added these words, "These are the only Jews among my fellow workers for the Kingdom of God..."[5] What Paul meant was that these were the only Jewish Christians to stand by Paul. What alienated most of the others was his persistence in accepting Gentiles into the Church without first requiring them to become Jews. That would have necessitated all Gentile males to be circumcised. Ernest Martin suggested that Paul must have felt very let down by this lack of support.[6] The Jewish Christians who opposed Paul's inclusivism felt that to be saved, one needed Jesus plus circumcision. Paul said, it's not Jesus plus anything; it's just Jesus.

One of our favorite texts undoubtedly is John 3:16 KJV: "For God so loved the world, that he gave his only begotten Son, that whosoever believeth in him should not perish, but have everlasting life." Filled with the Holy Spirit, the Apostle was reaching out to this lost world for which Christ Jesus had died. We, of course, can only speculate that if Paul's enemies had won their case and succeeded in imposing their vision on the fledgling faith, the Christian church would have remained just another sect of Judaism. However, thanks to the Pauline vision, the Christian faith was on the brink of becoming a world religion.

"These are the only Jews among my fellow workers for the kingdom of God, and they have proved a comfort to me."[7] Remember an incident in Moses' life. He was endeavoring to minister to all the Hebrew people all by himself: "The next day Moses took his seat to serve as judge for the people, and they stood around him from morning till evening. When his father-in-law saw all that Moses was doing for the people, he said, 'What is this you are doing for the people?" Why do you alone sit as judge, while all these people stand around you from morning till evening?'

"Moses answered him, 'Because the people come to me to seek God's will. Whenever they have a dispute, it is brought to me, and I decide between the parties and inform them of God's decrees and laws.' Moses father-in-law replied, 'What you are doing is not good." You and these people who come to you will only wear yourselves out. The work is too heavy for you; you cannot handle it alone...But select capable men from all the people - men who fear God, trustworthy men who hate dishonest gain...Have them serve as judges for the people... That will make your load lighter, because they will share it with you.'"[8] Think of the comfort they were to bring Moses. He wasn't in this alone.

How can you and I be a comfort for others? It strikes me that, in order to comfort others, we first have to be able to leave our own comfort zone. Billy Graham once quoted his own mother who said, "God doesn't comfort us to make us comfortable; He comforts us to make us comforters." I read this illustration: A man named Joe Bayly lost his little child. He said that he was just sitting alone, torn-up inside, when a would-be comforter sidled up beside him and proceeded to explain the child's passing and the promised hope beyond death. He quoted reams of scripture - which Joe could affirm. But none of it helped. He kept talking, and Joe just wanted him to go away, which he finally did Then someone else came and sat beside him, silently. He just listened to him, responded quietly, sat for over an hour, shared a short prayer, and left. Jim later said that it touched his heart, and he hated to see that person leave.[9]

When the armies of Babylon razed the Holy City to the ground, they carried much of the population away, to live as exiles in Babylon. The 137th Psalm begins with this lament, "By the rivers of Babylon we sat and wept, when we remembered Zion...How can we sing the songs of the Lord while in a foreign land?"[10] They sat down and wept, too despondent to do anything else. But the Lord Yahweh sent them a spokesman, the prophet Ezekiel, to comfort them. Ezekiel wrote, "I came to the exiles...And there, where they were living, I sat among them..."[11] That's all. He comforted them.

You too must learn to be a comforter. A brochure produced by the Billy Graham Evangelistic Association stated this challenge: Always remember that you may be the only light in someone's darkness.

Chapter 53: "Mature" (Col. 4:12 NIV)

I don't know how you feel about this, but when someone I hardly know sends their greetings, I feel non-plussed. Someone will say to me, "Oh, my grandmother's best friend's cousin, Joe Periwinkle, wants to be sure to tell you 'Hi!'". I usually answer, "That's sweet of him. Tell him I say 'Hi!' back." See, I don't even know him. But if someone I know sends greetings, that means a lot me in terms of their support and encouragement. So when Paul wrote to the Colossians and said, "Epaphras, who is one of you and a servant of Christ Jesus, sends greeting,"[1] that must have resonated with them.

He really was one of them and had a burden on his heart for them. He himself had founded the fellowship.[2] So you can imagine that he was personally invested in it. He was a servant of Christ Jesus because Jesus died to set him free. "And he died for all, that those who live should no longer live for themselves, but for him who died for them and was raised again."[3]

Epaphras "is always wrestling in prayer for you..."[4] As a teenager, my own life, attitudes, behaviors took many twists and turns. Years later, when I was pastoring a church, my Grandma Crossley confessed, "Every night of my life I prayed for Jerry, that the Lord would lead him into His service." So remember that you are where you are because someone was praying for you. There are such people in every church in every generation. We call them "prayer warriors."

In a church I served in Lancaster County, PA, there was one such woman. She had been the Sunday School teacher of an Adult Bible Class for decades. Pauline Wright had enriched the spiritual life of almost every member of our large congregation. She was so respected - even revered - that everyone referred to her as "Mother Wright". When I came as pastor to the church in 1987, that's what I called her, too. She was, in her retirement, the prayer warrior par excellence. One day, when I visited her, she picked up our church's pictorial directory and said to me, "I pray for each one of these people in this book every day." She prayed even for people she did not know. No wonder she was venerated by our congregation.

One of the most special statements you can make to someone is to say - and mean it - "I'm praying for you." The author of a devotional book made the following observation. He was reflecting on the fact that the Lord always sent him an Epaphras. He was always aware that this special person was in prayer for him, interceding before the throne of grace. His present Epaphras was now so helpless that he couldn't do anything - except pray. The author concluded with two searching questions. First, "Who is your Epaphras?" And, secondly, "Whose Epaphras are you?"[5]

Epaphras "is always wrestling in prayer for you, that you may stand firm in all the will of God, mature and fully assured."[6] We need to be mature, grown-up. As a pastor I've witnessed many examples of Christian immaturity. For one painful example, I once led a man to the Lord, only to hear him say one day, "Thanks, Jerry, for all your help. However, I want to tell you than I'm leaving your church." I was stunned. "Why are you leaving?" "Because I have to go where I will be fed." I can't even count the numbers of people who have left churches I pastored so that they could be "fed". At first I felt guilty because I figured that I was the culprit, that I was deficient as a Bible teacher. But, on second thought, I believe that the problem lay in them. I once heard another pastor say, "Too many Christians are far more interested in being fed than in feeding others. Too many immature Christians are looking for a bib when they ought to be looking for an apron." We need to care, in other words, less about being served, and more about serving.

My second example of Christian immaturity is generously provided by about a million people who obsessively hang onto their grudges and bitterness. I once wondered why they did that, what mileage they derived from nursing their hostility. Generally we don't do something unless there's a pay-off. So, what's the pay-off that we get from stirring up past grievances? Then it occurred to me: it strokes our feelings of self-righteousness, and self-righteousness feels good. Multitudes have said to me, "I stopped going to church because, one Sunday, someone said something so hurtful to me that I can never forget it." "When did that happen?" "Oh, about thirty years ago." I always want to say, and sometimes I do, "Get a life!"

Epaphras "is always wrestling in prayer for you, that you may stand firm in the will of God, mature and fully assured."[7] You will discover full assurance when you are in God's will. Dante Sagely said, "In His will is our peace."[8] Yet we foolishly persist in trying to fulfill our agenda, our plans for ourselves, our will. Then when we fail to find this fabled peace of God, we wind up feeling cheated. Honestly, we have been cheated, not by God but by ourselves. In His will - not ours - is our peace.

Chapter 54: "Give My Greetings" (Col. 4:15a NIV)

By the time Paul wrote his letter, the city of Colossae had already lost much of its glitter and glamor. It now was just a "has-been" town beside the Lycus River, a tributary of the Meander River. The twin cities of Laodicea and Hierapolis, nearby Colossae, were, by this time, far more important.[1] These three congregations were located in a valley within about ten miles of one another, so there was frequent contact between them.[2] Paul reminded them that his co-worker Epaphras had worked hard for all three congregations.[3]

Are we willing to work hard to share the Gospel with others? If it's "Good News" for me, if it's "Good News" for you, then it's "Good News" for them, too. William Booth once heard an atheist mocking the Christian faith. Zealously he proclaimed that if he himself seriously believed all this stuff about a Coming Judgment, and that unrepentant sinners would perish, then he would be willing to crawl on broken glass, with bare knees, all over the city of London to warn them. Those words, spoken by an atheist, made William Booth stop in his tracks and reflect on their truth. Those words served to turn William Booth into an evangelist and founder of the Salvation Army.[4]

Paul added two more names to his list: "Our dear friend Luke the doctor, and Demas send greetings."[5] "Luke, the doctor." On his second missionary journey, Paul had taken Luke with him as his personal physician.[6] One day, in the far future, this doctor would sit down and pen the third Gospel which has come down to us as "The Gospel According to St. Luke". He would also write the Book of Acts, the history book of the early church in which he would recount the acts of the Holy Spirit.

And it would be Luke who would see most clearly God's plan to bring the Gospel to the Gentiles. He would, for instance, record the words of Simeon, an old man awaiting the appearance of the Messiah. The Lord God had promised Simeon that he would see Him. I believe that Simeon was probably looking for a grown man, but when he caught a glimpse of the Christ-child, Simeon heard the Holy Spirit whisper, "This is He, this little baby." In ecstatic response Simeon fairly shouted, "Lord, now lettest thou thy servant depart in peace, according to thy word: for mine eyes have seen thy salvation, which thou hast prepared before the face of all people; a light to lighten the Gentiles, and the glory of thy people Israel." (Luke 2:29-31 KJV).

Luke saw ahead. Perhaps he saw God's Master Plan to bring salvation to the whole world. In Luke's gospel, the angel would say to the shepherds abiding in the field, "Fear not: for, behold, I bring you good tidings of great joy, which shall be to all people. For unto you is born this day in the city of David a Savior, which is Christ the Lord." (Luke 2:10-11 KJV).

"...and Demas sends greetings."[7] Paul curiously says nothing at all about him, except that he sends greetings. But in 2 Timothy we read, "Do your best to come to one quickly, for Demas, because he loved this world, has deserted me..."[8] Maybe Paul, when writing to the Colossians, was already a little suspicious of Demas because he didn't note anything favorable to say about him. Maybe he suspected that his ardor for the Master was already beginning to cool.[9]

I once had a best friend with a majestic solo voice. He was a powerful, Spirit-filled evangelist who consistently led people to Christ. Suddenly I heard that he had left simultaneously his ministry, his Lord, and his wife. Probably hundreds of people felt the same way I did: like I had just been punched in the stomach. This falling away from Jesus never remains a private affair; it generally involves many other people. Every day you and I have to make a decision: to walk with the Lord, or to walk away from Him. Remember the incident recorded in John 6? "From this time many of his disciples turned back and no longer followed him. 'You do not want to leave too, do you?' Jesus asked the twelve. Simon Peter answered him, 'Lord, to whom shall we go?' You have the words of eternal life.'"[10]

Recognizing that the congregation in Colossae was in constant contact with its sister churches, Paul wrote, "Give my greetings to...Laodicea, and to Nympha and the church in her house."[11] The very first Christians did not have church buildings, so they met in people's homes. They did not start building churches until the third century.[12] The Holy Spirit would use these followers of the Lord in dramatic ways to transform their world. We are living two millennia later, but we serve the same God. There's no telling how God will use us if we stand firm in Him.

Chapter 55: "See That it is Read" (Col. 4:16 NIV)

We are coming to the conclusion of Paul's letter. He writes, "After this letter has been read to you, see that it is also read in the church of the Laodiceans..."[1] "Have it read" means "read out loud to the whole congregation."[2] Then Paul added, "...and that you in turn read the letter from Laodicea."[3] Where is that letter? Did it survive? Is it in our Bible? The members of the congregation in Colossae were invited to exchange pastoral letters with each other. Laodicea was only around eleven miles away.

Some Bible scholars believe that the letter from Laodicea is in our Bible. It's Ephesians. These pastoral epistles were intended to be in circulation.[4] So what does this theological discourse mean for us today? That the "missing letter from Laodicea" is not missing at all! It actually is Ephesians. What's in our Bible is supposed to be there, and to survive, and to guide our footsteps. The prophet Isaiah wrote, "So is my word that goeth forth from my mouth: It will not return to me empty, but it will accomplish what I desire and achieve the purpose for which I sent it."[5]

The Apostle's next sentence was a reference to one of their own members. He said, "Tell Archippus: 'See to it that you complete the work you have received in the Lord.'"[6] In his letter to Philemon, Paul calls Archippus "our fellow soldier".[7] There will be those times when any sincere Christians will find themselves in battle. Whenever we actively endeavor to live out our Christian life, we're apt to find ourselves confronting sudden resistance and conflict. We wonder, "Where's all this flak coming from?" "Behind all of it may be a Satanic influence.

There's an instructive story that comes to us from the American Civil War. General Robert E. Lee, commander-in-chief of the armies of the Confederacy, sent a message to his subordinate, General "Stonewall" Jackson, to rendezvous with him. He mentioned that there wasn't anything particularly urgent to discuss. In fact, General Jackson was free to come at his own convenience.

It was teeming rain. General Robert E. Lee looked up and was shocked to see Stonewall Jackson galloping toward him at great speed. His commander-in-chief gently reminded him that he didn't have to show up right away. Jackson replied, "The slightest wish of my commander is a command that demands my instant obedience."[8] That should be our response to Jesus whenever we experience the promptings of the Holy Spirit.

"Complete the work." Well, most of us probably don't spend a lot of time contemplating the meaning and purpose of our life. We just live from day to day. However, in the course of my pastoral ministry I have met people who came very close to dying. They survived, and this became a watershed moment in their life. For one thing, it awakened them to their relationship with God. Typically, they'd say to me, "Jerry, I should have died. I don't know why I'm still here. The Lord must have interceded, and saved me for some reason. I believe that he spared me for a task. There's something that I'm still supposed to do." They display a new understanding of who they are and whose they are. They are not afraid to die; they are afraid to die without completing their task.

"Tell Archippus: See to it that you complete the work you have received in the Lord?"[9] This great God of the universe, who flung the myriad of galaxies into existence, and looks upon His earth, this "little blue dot", and sees you, has a plan for your life. In Romans we read these solemn words: "For none of us lives to himself alone and none of us dies to himself alone. If we live, we live to the Lord; and if we die, we die to the Lord. So, whether we live or die, we belong to the Lord."[10]

You must ask yourself, "What task does God want me to complete in His name? Is there someone He wants me to care for, share with, witness to?" Then you must lift that up in prayer and, in the silence, await the Lord's direction. You probably won't hear a tiny, squeaky voice, or even a thunderous voice. Instead, just a whisper, a sense of His leading. Wherever one door closes, another will open, and you'll experience yourself being led.

One man shared how, one day, he and his small son wandered into a field, filled with many weeds. Yet, in an obscure corner of the field they discovered a lovely patch of fragrant flowers. Even though they were surrounded by weeds, the flowers flourished, and lifted their blooms aloft. Now we've met people like that, people who perhaps lived out their lives unnoticed, tucked away in some far-off corner. Yet they unabashedly bore witness to their faith. When you and I come into His majestic presence, His question is not apt to be, "How many noticed you?", but, "Were you faithful where I placed you?"[11]

Chapter 56: "Grace be with You" (Col. 4:18 NIV)

"I, Paul, write this greeting in my own hand."[1] The author of the book, When God Whispers Your Name, Max Lucado, would write a wonderful passage expressing the irony of St. Paul's life. He would say something like this: Here was a pathetic man, locked up, awaiting execution. Who would believe that this helpless victim would shape the future of this world? or that his fame would outlive all the emperors? or that his thinking would influence curriculums? or that his pastoral letters, scratched on parchment, would one day be read in thousands of languages?[2] Who would believe it? Virtually nobody. But they'd be wrong, dead-wrong. "I, Paul..."

"I, Paul, write this greeting with my own hand."[3] Most of the letter to the Colossians had been written by Paul's secretary, for this is generally the way that Paul prepared the epistle.[4] His eyesight was very bad, so he dictated his letter. For instance, near the conclusion of his letter to the Romans, this line slipped in: "I, Tectius, who wrote down this letter, greet you in the Lord."[5] Now, at the conclusion of Colossians, Paul takes the pen and signs the letter himself "in my own hand". Why does he sign it himself? Because he wants to add a personal touch. His letter is intended to be intensely personal.

Then Paul adds, "Remember my chains."[6] His mention of "chains" was a subtle claim of authority. It went beyond a plea for sympathy. William Braclay wrote that it's as if Paul were saying, "Hey! This letter doesn't come from someone who doesn't know what he's talking about, from someone who tells you what to do while not being willing to do it himself. This letter is coming from someone who's been there and suffered for Christ."[7] He's saying, "I've been there. I haven't just 'talked the talk'; I've 'walked the walk'. I've been willing to put my life on the line. I have earned the right to be heard."

In the days of His flesh, Jesus had admonished his followers to be aware of the cost of discipleship. He said to them, "And anyone who does not carry his cross and follow me cannot be my disciple. Suppose one of you wants to build a tower. Will he not first sit down and estimate the cost to see if he has enough money to complete it?

For if he lays the foundation and is not able to finish it, everyone who sees it will ridicule him, saying, 'This fellow began to build and was not able to finish.'"[8] If you're toying with the thought of becoming a Christian, you have to remember that you're in it for the long-haul.

Paul's very last words in his pastoral letter were, "Grace be with you."[9] As was his custom, he concluded his correspondence with a blessing.[10] Grace! The free, unmerited gift of God's love. Curiously, if we turn to the very last book of the Bible, the Book of Revelation, and then the very last chapter, 22, and then the very last verse, 21 we read, "The grace of the Lord Jesus be with God's people. Amen."[11] So the very last sentence, not only in Colossians but also in the Bible itself, is this little word "grace". See, God Himself has the last word, and that word is "grace".[12] And it's also quite curious that this last word happens to be the first word in a Christian's life. Our spiritual journey begins with God's grace and ends with God's grace. Think of the beloved hymn:

"Amazing grace! How sweet the sound
That saved a wretch like me!
I once was lost, but now am found;
Was blind, but now I see.

"Twas grace that taught my heart to fear,
And grace my fears relieved.
How precious did that grace appear
The hour I first believed.

"Through many dangers, toils, and snares,
I have already come;
'tis grace hath brought me safe thus far,
And grace will lead me home."[13]

I want to conclude this devotional commentary with a poignant episode I read in a book entitled, "Let the Redeemed of the Lord Say So (Psalm 107:2). In a way, it's a story within a story. The authors were describing an incident in their ministry. They wrote that it occurred when they were attending an Evangelism Conference in Monterey, Mexico. Since there was a bilingual audience, all the lectures were presented in both Spanish and English. Professional translators worked simultaneously, and attendees wore headphones. One of the authors was giving a talk which utilized a legendary story well-known to many people: "Tie a Yellow Ribbon 'Round the Old Oak Tree".

In that story, a young man leaves home and falls into a self-destructive lifestyle that results in his incarceration. When his sentence is up, and it's time for his release, he writes a letter to his parents in which he acknowledges the shame he brought on them and the pain he gave to them. He tells them that he doesn't blame them if they don't ever want to see him again. But he wants them to know that he is being released. On a specified day and hour he'll be on a train that's heading back to his hometown. The tracks go right past their home, where there is a big oak tree that rises prominently behind the family home. Then he adds, "I don't want to embarrass you by getting off the train, walking to your home, and knocking on your front door. But if you want to see me, just tie a yellow ribbon around the old oak tree, and I'll see it as the train rounds the bend."

When that day arrives, with pounding pulse and racing heart, the young man boards the train but is too fearful even of looking out the window. He shares his story with his seatmate and asks him to look for the oak tree, and let him know if he spots a ribbon. As the train comes around the bend, the fellow traveler shouts to the young man, "Open your eyes, son; there's a yellow ribbon on every branch."

The author concluded, "Well, that's the story about the welcome our Heavenly Father will give the sinner who comes Home." Up to this moment, as the author was relating his story, he was constantly hearing the translator repeating it in Spanish. Suddenly, there were no words being spoken, Nothing was coming through the headphones Only silence. So the speaker naturally looked over at the translator who had stopped translating. He wasn't able to say anything. He had taken off his headset and was weeping. The translator suddenly understood the message of God's gracious forgiveness.[14] He himself had encountered God's unconditional love.

Just as I can. Just as you can. "Grace be with you." Amen.

END NOTES

Notes on the Introduction: All You Ever Need Is Jesus

1. Philippians and Colossians; J. Vernon McGee; Thomas Nelson Publishers; Nashville, TN; 1991; p.111.
2. Colossians: The Church's Lord and the Christian's Liberty; Ralph P. Martin; Zondervan Publishing House; Grand Rapids, Michigan 49506; ©1972 by The Paternoster Press; p.1.
3. Philippians and Colossians; F.C. Synge; SCM Press LTD; 56 Bloomsbury Street, London WC1; 1st published July 1951; reprinted June 1958; pp. 58-59.
4. Illustrations for Biblical Preaching; ed. by Michael P. Green; Baker Book House; Grand Rapids, Michigan 49516; ©1982, 1985, 1989 by Michael P. Green; "Apostasy, Development of, illus. #33, p. 23.
5. ¬1 Corinthians 15:1-2a NIV
6. Your Completeness in Christ; John MacArthur, Jr.; Moody Press, Chicago; 1984, 1985; p. 113 (published in association with the literary agency of Alive Communications; P.O. Box 49068, Colorado Springs, CO 80949).
7. Our Sufficiency in Christ; John MacArthur, Jr.; Word Publishing Company; Dallas, Texas; pp. 25-27.

Notes on Chapter 1: "Grace and Peace to You" (Colossians 1:2 NIV)

1. The Gospel in Hymns: Backgrounds and Interpretations; Albert Edward Bailey; Charles Scibner's Sons; New York; 1950; p. 126.
2. Ibid.; p. 127.
3. Ibid.; p.127 also.
4. Hymn "Amazing Grace"; John Newton; 1779 (1725-1807); vss. 1-3
5. Colossians 1:2 NIV
6. Studies in the Epistle to the Colossians; E. Schuyler English; Publication office "Our Hope" (Arno C. Gaebelein, Inc.); 456 Fourth Ave., New York, NY; 1944; p. 17.
7. Layman's Bible Book Commentary; Malcolm D. Tolbert; Broadman Press; Nashville, TN; 1980; p. 40.
8. Philippians 4:7 NIV

9. Believers Church Bible Commentary; Elmer A. Martens & Willard M. Swartley, Editors; "Colossians/Philemon" by Ernest D. Martin; Herald Press; Scottdale, PA 15683; 1993; p. 31-20. Great Archers and their Weapons and Fresh Arrows From Many Quivers: A Study of Illustrative Powers of Pulpit Orators, with selections of their Illustrations; Louis Albert Banks, D.D.; Published by F.M. Barton; Caxton Bldg.; Cleveland, Ohio; 1903; illus. #283, "With Christ in the Boat".

Notes on Chapter 2: "We Have Heard of Your Faith...and...Love" (Col. 1:4 NIV)

1. Col. 1:4a NIV
2. The Bible Exposition Commentary; vol. 2: Warren W. Wiersbe; Victor Books (A Division of Scripture Press Publications, Inc.); P.O. Box 1825, Wheaton, Illinois 60189; p. 107.
3. Col. 1:4a NIV
4. Macartney's Illustrations: Illustrations from the Sermons of Clarence Edward Macartney; Abingdon Press; NY & Nashville; 1945, 1946; p. 51c.
5. Col. 1:4 NIV
6. John 13:34-35 NIV
7. The MacArthur New Testament Commentary: Colossians & Philemon; John MacArthur, Jr.; Moody Press; Chicago; 1992; p. 19.
8. Luke 22:24-27 NIV
9. John 13:12-17 (paraphrase)
10. Matt. 9:36 NIV
11. Col. 1:4 NIV

Notes on Chapter 3: "The Hope that is Stored Up for You in Heaven" (Col. 1:5 NIV)

1. Col. 1:5a NIV
2. Jer. 29:11 NIV
3. INFO SEARCH; Published by The Computer Assistant; P.O. Box 151469, Arlington, Texas 76015; ©1986 through 1989 by Anthony D. Tooley; Illustrations on "Colossians" #828.
4. Hymn "God Moves in a Mysterious Way"; lyrics by William Cowper (1731-1800); vss. 1&5.

5. 1 Peter 1:3-4 NIV
6. Clippings from My Notebook: Writings and Sayings Collected by Corrie ten Boom; Thomas Nelson Publishers; Nashville, TN ©1982 by Christians Incorporated; "Good News," pp. 11-12.
7. Hymn "All the Way My Savior Leads Me"; lyrics by Fanny J. Crosby (1830-195); verse 3.

Notes on Chapter 4: "Bearing Fruit and Growing" (Col. 1:6 NIV)

1. Col. 1:6a NIV
2. Matt. 16:16-18 NIV
3. John 3:16
4. The Epistle to the Colossians; Roy Yates; Epworth Press; 1 Central Buildings, Westminster, London SW1H9 NA; 1993; p. 7.
5. In Him the Fullness: Homiletic Studies in Paul's Epistle to the Colossians; R.E.O. White; Fleming H. Revell Co., Old Tappan, NJ; 1973; p. 17.
6. Ibid.; p. 18.
7. Illustrations for Biblical Preaching; edited by Michael P. Green; Baker Book House; Grand Rapids, Michigan 49516; © 1982, 1985, 1989 by Michael P. Green; illustration #425, "Evangelism, Necessity For," p. 128.
8. 2 Timothy 2:9b NIV.

Notes on Chapter 5: "The Knowledge of His Will" (Col. 1:9 NIV)

1. Col. 1:7 NIV
2. The Bible Exposition Commentary; vol. 2; Warren W. Wiersbe; Victor Books (A Division of SP Publications Inc.), P.O. Box 1825, Wheaton, Illinois 60189; 1989, p. 107.
3. You are Loved & Forgiven: Paul's Letter of Hope to the Colossians; Lloyd John Ogilvie; Regal Books (A Division of GL Publications); Ventura, California; 1977; P. 16.
4. Colossians: The Church's Lord and the Christian's Liberty; Ralph P. Martin; Zondervan Publisher Company; Grand Rapids, Michigan 49506; ©1972 by The Paternoster Press; p. 25.
5. Romans 10:12-14a NIV
6. Col. 1:7 NIV
7. Luke 18:8 NIV

8. Rev. 2:10b NIV
9. Col. 1:9a NIV
10. Col. 1:9b NIV
11. The Letters to the Philippians, Colossians, and Thessalonians; The Daily Study Bible Series, rev. ed.; William Barclay; The Westminster Press; Philadelphia; 1975; p. 108.
12. Encyclopedia of 7,700 Illustrations: Signs of the Times; Paul Lee Tan, ThD.; Assurance Publishers; P.O. Box 753, Rockville, Maryland 20851: ©1979 by Paul Lee Tan; Illustration #6111, "Nothing Else," p. 1368.

Notes on Chapter 6: "Live a Life Worthy of the Lord" (Col. 1:10 NIV)

1. Micah 6:6-8 NIV
2. Col. 1:10 NIV
3. Col. 1:9 NIV
4. Layman's Bible Book Commentary, Philippians, Colossians, 1 & 2 Thessalonians, 1 & 2 Timothy, Titus, Philemon; vol. 22; Malcom O. Tolbert; Broadman Press; Nashville, Tenn.; 1980; p. 42.
5. Eph. 4:1 NIV
6. The Epistle to the Colossians: A study manual; Charles N. Pickell; Baker Book House; Grand Rapids, Michigan 49516; 1965; p. 31.
7. INFO SEARCH; Published by the Computer Assistant; P.O. Box 151469, Arlington, Texas 76015; ©1986 through 1989 by Anthony D. Tooley; Illustrations on "Colossians"; Illus. #702. "The Supreme Motive".
8. Col. 1:10 NIV
9. Gal. 1:10 NIV
10. Spiritual Intimacy; Richard Mayhue; Victor Books (A Division of Scripture Press Publications, Inc.); 1825 College Ave., Wheaton, Ill 60187; 1990; p. 150.
11. Heb. 13:20-21 NIV
12. Col. 1:10 NIV
13. Jer. 9:23-24a NIV
14. The Prayer Factor; Sammy Tippit; Moody Press; Chicago; 1988; ©1988 by the Moody Bible Institute of Chicago; p.40 (Italics mine).

Notes on Chapter 7: "Share in the Inheritance of the Saints" (Col. 1:12 NIV)

1. Col. 1:11 NIV
2. Eph. 6:10 NIV
3. 2 Cor. 12:9 NIV
9. Bible Illustrator (For IBM PC and Compatible Computers); Parsons Technology, Inc.; One Parsons Drive, P.O. Box 100, Hiawatha, Iowa 52233-0100; ©1990-1992 by Parsons Technology, Inc.; illus. #323; index 3808-3811, "God, Power of".
5. Col. 1:11 NIV
6. Macartney's Illustrations: Illustrations from the Sermons of Clarence Edward Macartney; Abingdon Press; NY & Nashville; ©1945 by Whitmore & Stone; p. 52.
7. Matt. 18:20 NIV
8. INFO SEARCH; published by The Computer Assistants, P.O. Box 151469, Arlington, Texas 76015 ©1986 through 1989 by Anthony D. Tooley; Illustrations on "Colossians," illus. #24, "How Wesley Learned to Praise".
9. Col. 1:12a NIV
10. INFO SEARACH; op. cit.; "The Salt of Gratitude".
11. Col. 1:12 NIV
12. The Epistle to the Colossians: A Study Manual; Charles N. Pickell; Baker Book House; Grand Rapids, Michigan 49516; 1965; p. 32.
13. John 14:2a-3 NIV
14. Joy Wider than the World: A Teaching & Preaching Commentary on Philippians; Ron James; Upper Room Books; The Upper Room; 1908 Grand Avenue, P.O. Box 189, Nashville, TN 37202; ©1992 by Ron James; p. 105.
15. Cor. 2:9 NIV

Notes on Chapter 8: "The Kingdom of the Son" (Col. 1:13 NIV)

1. Col. 1:13 NIV
2. Hymn "Praise, My Soul, the King of Heaven", Henry F. Lyte (1793-1847); written 1834; v. 1.
3. Col. 1:13a NIV

4. The Mind of St. Paul; William Barclay; Harper & Row, Publishers, Inc.; 10 East 53rd St., New York, NY 10022; ©1958 by Wm. Barclay; © renewed 1986 by Ronald Barclay; p. 84.
5. Our Sufficiency in Christ; John MacArthur, Jr.; Word Publishing Company; Dallas, Texas; 1991; pp. 141-12.
6. Ibid.; pp 142-144.
7. Col. 1:13 NIV
8. INFO SEARCH; published by The Computer Assistant, P.O. Box 151469, Arlington, Texas 76015; ©1986 through 1989 by Anthony D. Tooley; Illustrations on Colossians; "Rags for a Robe"
9. Isa. 64:6a NIV
10 1 Peter 2:9 NIV

Notes on Chapter 9: "Redemption" (Col. 1:14 NIV)

1. Col. 1:13-14 NIV
2. Understanding Jesus: Who Jesus Christ Is and Why He Matters; Alister McGrath; Academic Books; Zondervan Publishing House; 1415 Lake Drive, S.E., Grand Rapids, Michigan 49506; 1987; p. 126.
3. 1 Cor. 6:19b-20a NIV
4. 1 Peter 1:18a, 19a NIV
5. The Blood; Benny Hinn; Creation House; Strang Communications Company; 600 Rinehart Rd., Lake Mary, Fl. 32746; 1993; pp. 105-106.
6. Isaiah 44:22 NIV
7. The Old Farmer's Almanac 1995; Robert B. Thomas; The Old Farmer's Almanac; Dublin, NH 03444; 1995; article "E-MC2, So What?" by Michael McNiemey; pp. 112-113.
8. How to be Pentecostal Without Speaking in Tongues; Tony Campolo; Word Publishing Company; Dallas, Texas; 1991; pp. 86-87.

Notes on Chapter 10: "He is the Image of the Invisible God" (Col. 1:15a NIV)

1. Col. 1:15a NIV

2. Was Jesus Who He Said He Was? Michael Green; Vine Books (an imprint of Servant Books); P.O. Box 8617, Ann Arbor, Michigan 48107 ©1983 by Michael Green; p. 82.
3. The Christian Agnostic; Leslie D. Weatherhead; Abingdon Press; Nashville, Tennessee; 1965; p. 40.
4. Col. 1:15a NIV
5. INFO SERARCH; The Computer Assistant; P.O. Box 151469, Arlington, Texas 76015; ©1986 through 1989 by Anthony D. Tooley; Illustrations on Colossians.
6. Illustrations for Biblical Preaching; edited by Michael P. Green; Baker Book House; Grand Rapids, Michigan 49516; ©1982, 1985, 1989 by Michael P. Green; "God's Invisibility," illus. #576, p. 168.
7. Basic Christianity; John R.W. Stott; Inter-Varsity Press; Downers Grove, Illinois 60515; 1956; p. 14.
8. John 1:1-13 NIV
9. John 1:14, 18 NIV
10. Understanding Jesus: Who Jesus Christ Is and Why He Matters; Alister McGrath; published by Academic Books, Zondervan Publishing House; 1415 Lake Drive, S.E., Grand Rapids, Michigan 49506; 1987; pp. 112-113.
11. 2 Corinthians 4:6 NIV

Notes on Chapter 11: "For by Him All Things were Created" (Col. 1:16 NIV)

1. Philippians Colossians Philemon; Harlyn J. Kuschel; People's Bible Commentary; Concordia Publishing House; 3558 S. Jefferson Ave., St. Louis, MO 63118-3968; 1992; p. 124.
2. Hebrews 1:1-3a NIV
3. The Faithful Christian: An Anthology of Billy Graham; compiled by William Griffin and Ruth Graham Dienert; McCracken Press; 575 Madison Ave., Suite 1006, New York, NY 10022; Multi Media Communicators, Inc.; 1994; p. 13.
4. Col. 1:15a, 16a, 17 NIV
5. John 8:53-58 NIV
6. Disappointment with God: Three Questions to One Asks Aloud; Philip Yancey; Zondervan Publishing House; 1415 Lake Drive, S.E., Grand Rapids, MI 49506; 1988; pp. 195-196.
7. Col. 1:17 NIV

8. Psalm 147:3-4 NIV
9. Psalm 138:6a NIV

Notes on Chapter 12: "Supremacy" (Col. 1:18c NIV)

1. INFO SEARCH; Published by The Computer Assistant; P.O. Box 151469, Arlington, Texas 76015; ©1986 thru 1989 by Anthony D. Tooley; Illustrations on "Colossians", #1078: A Big Savior.
2. Col. 1:18 NIV
3. The All-Sufficient Christ: Studies in Paul's letter to the Colossians; Wm. Barclay; The Westminster Press; Philadelphia; 1963; pp. 111-112.
4. Encyclopedia of 7,700 Illustrations; Signs of the Times; Paul Lee Tan, Th.D..; Assurance Publishers; P.O. Box 753, Rockville, Maryland 20851; ©1979 by Paul Leo Tan; Illus. #820, "Take All the Keys, Lord;" p. 270.
5. INFO SEARCH; op. cit.; "Who Gets Center Stage?"
6. Ibid.; "At His Feet" & Knight's Master Book of New Illustrations; Walter B. Knight; Wm. B. Eerdmans Publishing Company; Grand Rapids, Michigan 49503; 1956; ©1956 by Wm. B. Eerdmans Publishing Company; "Every Knee Shall Bow," p. 33b.
7. Philippians 2:9-11 NIV

Notes on Chapter 13: "All His Fullness" (Col. 1:19 NIV)

1. Knight's Master Book of New Illustrations; Walter B. Knight; Wm. B. Eerdmans Publishing Company; Grand Rapids, Michigan 49503; ©1956 Eerdmans; "Have You Ever Heard Such?"; p. 328.
2. John 15:5 NIV
3. Col. 1:19 NIV
4. Hymn "I Know Not How that Bethlehem's Babe"; Harry Webb Farrington, 1880-1931; (all verses).
5. John 1:1-2,14 NIV
6. Illustrations for Biblical Preaching; edited by Michael P. Green; Baker Book House; Grand Rapids, Michigan 49516; ©1982, 1985, 1989 by Michael P. Green; Illus. #128, "Christ, Incarnation of," p. 48.
7. John 14:6-9a NIV

8. A Scientific Approach to Biblical Mysteries; Robert W. Faid; New Leaf Press, Inc. P.O. Box 311, Green Forest, AR 72638; June 1993; "Understanding the Trinity," p. 176.

Notes on Chapter 14: "Peace Through His Blood" (Col. 1:20b NIV)

1. Hymn "There is a Fountain Filled with Blood"; William Cowper (1731-1800); written ©1771; verse 1.
2. Ibid.; v. 3.
3, INFO SEARCH; published by The Computer Assistant; P.O. Box 151467, Arlington, Texas 76015; ©1968 through 1989 by Anthony D. Tooley; (Illustrations on "Colossians").
4. Romans 5:6-8 NIV
5. Col. 1:19-20a NIV
6. 2 Corinthians 5:19a NIV
7. This incident took place around 1955. "Stosh" was Stanley Dlugosz, and he was an usher in our wedding on June 25, 1960.
8. Col. 1:20 NIV
9. Come With Faith; Michael Daves; Abingdon Press; NY & Nashville; 1964; pp. 47-48.

Notes on Chapter 15: "Without Blemish" (Col. 1:22 NIV)

1. "Invictus"; William Ernest Henley; 1875
2. Col. 1:21 NIV
3. Isa. 59:1-2 NIV
4. John 3:19 NIV
5. Minister's Manual (Doran's); sixty fifth Annual Issue; 1990 edition; edited by James W. Cox; Harper & Row, Publishers, Inc.; 10 East 53rd St., New York, NY 10022; "Our True Salvation," p. 167.
6. Col. 1:22b NIV
7. Col. 1:23a NIV
8. 2 Timothy 4:6-8 NIV
9. The origin of this story is unknown to me.

Notes on Chapter 16: "Rejoice in What Was Suffered" (Col. 1:24 NIV)

1. Matt. 16:24-25 NIV

2. Col. 1:24a NIV
3. 2 Corinthians 11:23b-27 NIV
4. Col. 1:24a NIV
5. Matt. 5:11-12 NIV
6. The Interpreter's Bible; Vol. 11; General Editor Nolan B. Harmon; Abingdon Press; "Colossians," exposition by G. Preston MacLeod; NY & Nashville, TN, 1955; p. 177.
7. Philippians 1:29 NIV
8. Acts 9:15-16 NIV
9. Illustrations for Biblical Preaching; edited by Michael P. Green; Baker Book House; Grand Rapids, Michigan 49516; ©1982, 1985, 1989 by Michael P. Green; illustration #1482, p. 402. (From Queen of the Dark Chamber by Christiana Tsai)

Notes on Chapter 17: "The Mystery" (Col. 1:26 NIV)

1. Col. 1:25 NIV
2. Isaiah 60:1-3 NIV
3. Col. 1:25-26b NIV
4. Proclaiming the New Testament; vol. 4; The Epistles to the Philippians, Colossians, and Philemon; Paul S. Rees; Baker Book House; Grand Rapids, Michigan; 1964, p. 79.
5. John 3:16
6. Col. 1: 26 NIV
7. Matt. 10:26-27 NIV
8. John 1:10-13 NIV
9. Daily Guideposts; Guideposts Associates, Inc.; Carmel, NY 10512; 1990; story told by Marilyn Morgan Helleberg; pp. 202-203.

Notes on Chapter 18: "Christ in You, the Hope of Glory" (Col. 1:27 NIV)

1. Col. 1:27a NIV
2. Acts 15:8-9, 11 NIV
3. Hymn "In Christ There is No East or West"; John Oxenham (1852-1941); written 1908; v. 1.
4. Col. 1:27a, b NIV
5. Luke 2:29-32 NIV
6. Col. 1:27a, b, c NIV (Italics mine)

7. Ring of Truth; A Translator's Testimony; J.B. Phillips; The Macmillan Co.; New York; 1967; p. 41.
8. You Are Loved & Forgiven: Paul's Letter of Hope to the Colossians; Lloyd John Ogilvie; Regal Books (A Division of GL Publications; Ventura, California; 1977; p. 75.
9. Col. 1:27d NIV
10. The Message: The New Testament in Contemporary Language; Eugene H. Peterson; Nav Press; P.O. Box 35001, Colorado Springs, CO 80935; ©1993 by Eugene Peterson; p. 498.

Notes on Chapter 19: "We Proclaim Him" (Col. 1:28a NIV)

1. Col. 1:28a NIV (Italics mine)
2. Lectures on the Epistle to the Colossians; H.A. Ironside; Loizeaux Brothers, Publisher; 1 East 13th St. New York, NY; 1928; p. 59.
3. Knight's Up-To-The-Minute Illustrations; Walter B. Knight; Moody Press; Chicago; ©1974 by The Moody Bible Institute of Chicago; p. 190; "No Choice".
4. Col. 1:28a, b NIV
5. Communicator's Commentary; Lloyd J. Ogilvie, General Editor; vol. 8 by Maxie D. Dunman; Word Books, Publisher; Waco, Texas; 1982; pp. 363-364
6. 1 Corinthians 1:20-25 NIV
7. Col. 1:28c NIV
8. Rom. 8:29a NIV
9. INFO SEARCH; published by The Computer Assistant; P.O. Box 151469, Arlington, Texas 76015; ©1986 through 1989 by Anthony D. Tooley; Illustrations on "Colossians," #1731, "The Weak Empowered".

Notes on Chapter 20: "To This End I Labor" (Col. 1:29 NIV)

1. Col. 1:28b-29 NIV
2. From a brochure I once read: What Does It Mean to Believe? by Oswald J. Smith; published by the Peoples Church, Toronto; 374 Shepard Avenue East, Willowdale, Ontario, Canada M2N3B6 (date?).

Notes on Chapter 21: "The Mystery of God" (Col. 2:2 NIV)

1. Col. 2:1 NIV
2. The Letters to the Philippians, Colossians, and Thessalonians; The Daily Study Bible Series; rev. ed.; William Barclay; The Westminster Press; Philadelphia; 1975; p. 128.
3. James 5:16b NIV
4. Col. 2:2a NIV
5. The Sole Sufficiency of Jesus Christ: Studies in the Epistle to the Colossians; Herbert W. Craggs, published by Marshall, Morgan & Scott, LTD; 1-5 Portpool Lane, Hoborn, E.C.I., London; ©1961 by Herbert W. Cragg; p. 48.
6. John 17:21 NIV
7. Col. 2:2b-3 NIV

Notes on Chapter 22: "How From Your Faith" (Col. 2:5b NIV)

1. Col. 2:4 NIV
2. Col. 2:4a NIV
3. Col. 2:4b NIV
4. New Courage for Daily Living: Devotions for Adults; Martin H. Franzmann; Concordia Publishing House; St. Louis, Missouri; 1963; p. 29.
5. You are Loved & Forgiven: Paul's Letter of Hope to the Colossians; Lloyd John Ogilvie; Regal Books (A Division of GL Publications); Ventura, California; 1977; p. 91.
6. Knight's Treasury of Illustrations; Walter B. Knight; Wm. B. Eerdmans Publishing Company; Grand Rapids, Michigan 49503; ©1963 by Wm. B. Eerdmans Publishing Company's; p. 181 (From "The Alliance Witness").
7. Col. 2:5 NIV
8. The Letters to the Philippians, Colossians, and Thessalonians; The Daily Study Bible Series; rev. ed.; William Barclay; The Westminster Press; Philadelphia; 1975; p. 131.
9. Philippians and Colossians; J. Vernon McGee; Thomas Nelson Publishers; Nashville, TN; 1991; p. 153.
10. Col. 2:5 NIV
11. INFO SEARCH; published by The Computer Assistant; P.O. Box 151469, Arlington, Texas 76015; ©1986 thru 1989 by Anthony D. Tooley; (Illustrations on "Colossians"); #1396: "Leave the Results to God."

12. Encyclopedia of 7,7000 Illustrations: Signs of the Times; Paul Lee Tan, ThD.; Assurance Publishers; P.O. Box 753, Rockville, Maryland 20851; illus. #1881, "That Boy in Organ Loft," p. 482.
13. 1 Corinthians 15:58b NIV

Notes on Chapter 23: "Strengthened in the Faith" (Col. 2:7 NIV)

1. Col. 2:6 NIV
2. INFO SEARCH; published by The Computer Assistant; P.O. Box 151469, Arlington, Texas 76015; ©1986 thru 1989 by Anthony D. Tooley; Illustration #965, "A Gift to be Received."
3. Col. 2:6 NIV
4. Daybreak: Daily Devotions from Acts and the Pauline Epistles; John T. Seamands; ©1993 by John T. Seamands; 407 Talbott Drive, Wilmore, KY 40390; meditation for October 20.
5. John 15:5 NIV
6. Col. 2:6-7a NIV
7. Studies in Colossians: The Pre-Eminent Christ; Richard Sturz; Moody Press; Chicago; 1955; p. 69.
8. Growing Strong in the Seasons of Life; Charles R. Swindoll; Multnomah Press; Portland, Oregon 97266; 1983; pp. 115-116.
9. Col. 2:6-7 NIV
10. Hymn "My Hope is Built"; words by Edward Mote, 1834; verse 2.

Notes on Chapter 24: "All the fullness of the Deity" (Col. 2:9 NIV)

1. Col. 2:6
2. Colossians and Philemon: The Supremacy of Christ; R. Kent Hughes; Crossway Books; Westchester, Illinois 60154 (A Division of Good News Publishers); ©1989 by R. Kent Hughes; p. 68.
3. Col. 2:8a NIV
4. Our Sufficiency in Christ; John MacArthur, Jr.; Word Publishing Company; Dallas, Texas; 1991; p. 172.
5. Lectures on the Epistle to the Colossians; H.A. Ironside; Loizeaux Brothers, Publishers; 1 East 13th St., New York, NJ; 1928; p. 67.
6. How to be a Christian in an UnChristian World; Fritz Ridenour; published by Regal Books (A Division of G/L Publications; Glendale, California 91209; 1971; p. 74.

7. The Letters to the Philippians, Colossians, and Thessalonians; The Daily Study Bible Series; rev. ed.; Wm. Barclay; the Westminster Press; Philadelphia; 1975; p. 134.
8. Col. 2:9 NIV
9. Rev. Dr. Armstrong, Ursinus College, ©1957
10. John 14:8-9 NIV
11. Mark 2:1-4 NIV
12. Mark 2:5-7 NIV
13. Mark 2:8-9 NIV
14. Mark 2:10-12 NIV
15. Eucharistic Hymn, "Let All Mortal Flesh Keep Silence," words from the Liturgy of St. James, 4th century; trans. by Gerard Moultrie, 1864

Notes on Chapter 25: "Fullness in Christ" (Col. 2:10 NIV)

1. This incident took place at a Full Gospel Businessmen's Fellowship International (FGBMFI) Dinner, somewhere ©1970, in Trevose, PA.
2. Col. 2:9 NIV
3. Col. 2:10a NIV
4. John 15:5 NIV
5. The Bible Exposition Commentary; vol. 2; Warren W. Wiersbe; Victor Books (A Division of Scripture Press Publications, Inc.); P.O. Box 1825, Wheaton, Illinois 60189; 1989; pp. 104-105.
6. Col. 2:10 NIV
7. Matt. 28:18 NIV
8. Philipp. 2:9-11 NIV

Notes on Chapter 26: "Buried with Him...Raised with Him" (Col. 2:12 NIV)

1. Gen. 17:9, 10b, 11b NIV
2. Col. 2:11a NIV
3. Deut. 10:16 NIV (Italics mine)
4;. Deut. 30:6 NIV (Italics mine)
5. Jer. 4:4b NIV (Italics mine)
6. Rom. 2:28-29a NIV (Italics mine)
7. Col. 2:11-12 NIV

8. Colossians: The Church's Lord and the Christian's Liberty; Ralph P. Martin; Zondervan Publishing House; Grand Rapids, Michigan 49506; ©1972 by The Paternoster Press; p.76.
9. The Letters to the Philippians, Colossians, and Thessalonians; The Daily Study Bible Series; rev. ed.; Wm. Barclay; The Westminster Press; Philadelphia; 1975; p. 140.
10. The All-Sufficient Christ: Studies in Paul's Letter to the Colossians; Wm. Barclay; The Westminster Press; Philadelphia; 1963; p. 91.
11. Romans 6:3-4 NIV
12. The Pilgrim's Progress: John Bunyan; Christian Literature Crusade; Fort Washinton, PA.; 1963; p. 46.
13. Hymn "Alas! and Did My Savior Bleed"; words by Isaac Watts; 1707; refrain by Ralph E. Hudson; 1885

Notes on Chapter 27: "He Forgave Us" (Col. 2:13b NIV)

1. The Letters to the Philippians, Colossians, and Thessalonians; The Daily Study Bible Series; rev. ed.; Wm. Barclay; The Westminster Press; Philadelphia; 1975; p. 141.
2. Col. 2:13b-14a NIV
3. Col. 2:13 NIV
4. Your Completeness in Christ. John MacArthur, Jr.; Moody Press; Chicago; 1984, 1985; published in association with the literary agency of Alive Communications; P.O. Box 49068, Colorado Springs, CO 80949; p. 103.
5. Decision Magazine; Billy Graham Evangelistic Association; 1300 Harmon Place, P.O. Box 779, Minneapolis, Minnesota 55440-0779; Vol. 37, No. 3, March 1996; article "The Cry of Our Hearts," Nigel Lee; p. 27.
6. Hymn "O For a Thousand Tongues to Sing"; Charles Wesley (1739); vss. 1, 3 & 4.

Notes on Chapter 28: "Nailing It to the Cross" (Col. 2:14b NIV)

1. Col. 2:13-14 NIV
2. Isa. 43:25 NIV
3. Jer. 31:31,33b, 34b NIV
4. Micah 7:19 NIV
5. Psalm 103:8-14 NIV

6. Isa. 40:1-2 NIV
7. The Christian Agnostic; Leslie D. Weatherhead; Abingdon Press, Nashville, NY; 1965; p. 194
8. Col. 2:14c NIV
9. Isa. 53:5-6 NIV
10 Hymn "It is Well with My Soul"; Horatio G. Spafford; 1873; v. 3.

Notes on Chapter 29:"Triumphing" (Col. 2:15b NIV)

1. Col. 2:15b NIV
2. Col. 2:15A NIV
3. Jn. 19:30 NIV
4. Hymn "Christ the Lord is Risen Today"; Charles Wesley; 1739; verse 2.
5. The Sole Sufficiency of Jesus Christ: Studies in the Epistle to the Colossians; Herbert W. Cragg; Marshall, Morgan & Scott, LTD; 1-5 Portpool Lane, Holborn, E.C.I., London; ©1961 by Herbert W. Cragg; p. 61.
6. Col. 2:15b NIV
7. The Letter to the Philippians, Colossians, and Thessalonians: The Daily Study Bible Series; rev. ed.; Wm. Barclay; The Westminster Press, Philadelphia; 1975; p. 143.
8. Col. 2:15b NIV
9. Marcartney's Illustrations: Illustrations from the Sermons of Clarence Edward Macartney; Abingdon Press; NY & Nashville; ©1946 by Stone & Pierce; p. 54.
10. Daniel 7:14b NIV
11. 2 Cor. 4:18 NIV
12. Rom. 8:37-39 NIV

Notes on Chapter 30: "The Reality...is Found in Christ" (Col. 2:17b NIV)

1. Col. 2:16-17 NIV
2. Colossians: The Church's Lord and the Christian's Liberty; Ralph P. Martin; Zondervan Publishing Company; Grand Rapids, Michigan 49506; ©1973 Paternoster Press; p. 90.
3. Mark 7:14-16, 20-23 NIV
4. Rom. 14:17 NIV
5. Col. 2: 16b NIV

6. Mk. 2:27 NIV
7. Col. 2:17 NIV
8. Evidence that Demands a Verdict; vol. 1: Historical Evidences for the Christian Faith; John McDowell; Thomas Nelson Publishers; Nashville (Published by Here's Life Publishers, Inc.; P.O. Box 1576, San Bernardino, CA 92402; ©1972, 1979 by Campus Crusade for Christ, Inc.) pp. 363-365

Notes on Chapter 31: "Do Not Let Anyone Disqualify You" (Col. 2:18 NIV

1. Col. 2:18 NIV
2. Layman's Bible Book Commentary; vol. 22; Malcolm O. Tolbert; Broadman Press; Nashville, TN; 1980; p. 51.
3. The Bible Exposition Commentary; vol. 2; Warren W. Wiersbe; Victor Books (A Division of Scripture Press Publications, Inc.); P.O. Box 1825, Wheaton, Illinois 60189; 1989; p. 130.
4. Paul and the Intellectuals: The Epistle to the Colossians; A.T. Roberston; rev. and ed. by W.C. Strickland; Broadman Press; Nashville, TN; 1956, p. 89.
5. Col. 2:18 NIV
6. Hard Sayings of the Bible; Walter C. Kaiser, Jr., Peter H. Davids, F.F. Bruce, Manfred T. Brauch; Inter Varsity Press; P.O. Box 1400, Downers Grove, Ill. 60515; © 1996 by Walter C. Kaiser, Tr., Peter H. David," F.F. Bruce & Manfred T. Brauch; p. 657.
7. Ibid.; p. 658
9. Studies in Colossians and Philemon; William Henry Griffith Thomas, D.D.; Baker Book House; Grand Rapids, Michigan 49516; 1973, 1974; p. 96
10. 1 Timothy 2:5-6a NIV
11. John 10:9a NIV
12. Hymn, "Spirit of God, Descend Upon My Heart," George Croly; 1867; v. 2.
13. John 15:5
14. 2 Peter 3:18 NIV

Notes on Chapter 32: "As Though You Still Belonged to [this World]" (Col. 2:20 NIV)

1. Col. 2:20 NIV

2. The Bible Exposition Commentary; vol. 2; Warren W. Wiersbe; Victor Books (A Division of Scripture Press Publications, Inc. P.O. Box 1825; Wheaton, Illinois 60189, 1979 p. 131.
3. Col. 2:22
4. John 13:34-35 NIV
5. INFO SEARCH; published by The Computer Assistant; P.O. Box 151469, Arlington, Texas 76015; ©1986 through 1989 by Anthony D. Tooley; Illustrations on Colossians; "Just Like Jesus."

Notes on Chapter 33: "Set Your Hearts on Things Above" (Col. 3:1 NIV)

1. Col. 3:1a NIV
2. Studies in the Epistle to the Colossians; E. Schuyler English; Publication Office "Our Hope" (Arno C. Garbelein, Inc.); 456 Fourth Ave., New York, NY; 1944; p. 91.
3. How to be a Christian in an UnChristian World; Fritz Redenour; Regal Books (A Division of G/L Publications; Glendale, Calif. 91209; 1971; back cover.
4. Col. 3:1a NIV
5. Eph. 2:40-6 NIV
6. Col. 3:1-2 NIV
7. Knight's Master Book of New Illustrations; Walter B. Knight; Wm. B. Eerdmans Publishing Company; Grand Rapids, Michigan 49503; ©1956 by Wm. B. Eerdmans Publishing Company; "Loaded Down with Harmless Things!" p. 749; C. Ray Angell.
8. INFO SEARCH; published by The Computer Assistant; P.O. Box 151469, Arlington, Texas 76015; ©1986 through 1989 by Anthony D. Tooley; illus. #1409, "Weighed Down or Way Up?"
9. Heb. 12:1-2 NIV
10. INFO SEARCH; op. cit.; illus. #736; "The Snails of Sin".
11. Hymn "Give Me Jesus"; Anny J. Crosby; vss. 1&4

Notes on Chapter 34: "Your Life in Now Hidden with Christ" (Col. 3:3 NIV)

1. Col. 3:2-3 NIV

2. The Bible Exposition Commentary; vol. 2; Warren W. Wiersbe; Victor Books, A Division of Scripture Press Publications, Inc.; P.O. Box 1825; Wheaton, Illinois 60189; p. 133.
3. Col. 3:3 NIV
4. Ps. 27:5,1 NIV
5. Minsters Manual (Doran's); 65th Annual Issue; 1990 Edition; ed. by James W. Cox; Harper & Row, Publishers; Sand Francisco, ©1989 by James W. Cox; p. 148, "Bold Confession".
6. Col. 3:4 NIV
7. Mk. 13:26 NIV
8. INFO SEARCH; published by The Computer Assistant; P.O. Box 151469, Arlington, Texas 76015; ©1986 through 1989 by Anthony D. Tooley; #621, "Waiting for the Son".
9. Ibid.; "1175, "It's Later than ever Before!".
10. Col. 3:4 NIV
11. Jn. 12:26a NIV
12. Jn. 14:19 NIV
13. 1 Cor. 2:9 NIV (Quoting Isa. 64.4)

Notes on Chapter 35: "The Life You Once Lived" (Col. 3:7 NIV)

1. Col. 3:5a NIV
2. Studies in Colossians: The Pre-eminent Christ; Richard Sturz; Moody Press; Chicago; 1955; p. 94.
3. Matt. 5:29-30 NIV
4. Rom. 6:3-4 NIV
5. Rom. 6:11 NIV
6. Bible Illustrator; Parsons Technology Inc.; One Parsons Drive, P.O. Box 100, Hiawatha, Iowa 52233-0100; ©1990-1992 by Parson Technology, Inc.; Index #2139, "Bondaye -Spiritual", p. 55.
7. Philippians and Colossians; J. Vernon McGee; Thomas Nelson, Publishers; Nashville, TN; 1991; p. 169.
8. Col. 3:6
9. Believers Church Bible Commentary; NT editors Willard M. Swartley & Howard H. Charles; "Colossians, Philemon" by Earnest D. Martin; Herald Press; Scottsday, PA 15683; 1993; p. 164.
10. Col. 3:7 NIV

11. INFO SEARCH; Published by The Computer Assistant; P.O. Box 151469, Arlington, Texas 76015; ©1986 through 1989 by Anthony D. Tooley; illus. #207, "The Wonderful Change".

Notes on Chapter 36: "Put on the New Self" (Col. 3:10 NIV)

1. Heb. 12:1 NIV
2. Col. 3:8 NIV
3. Col. 3:9-10 NIV
4. Colossians: The Church's Lord and the Christian's Liberty; Ralph P. Martin; Zondervan Publishing House; Grand Rapids, Michigan 49506; ©1972 by The Paternoster Press; P. 111.
5. The Letters to the Philippians, Colossians, and Thessalonians; The Daily Study Bible Series; rev. ed.; William Barclay; The Westminster Press; Philadelphia; ©1975 by William Barclay; p. 152.
6. Rom. 6:4b NIV
7. INFO SEARCH; published by The Computer Assistant; P.O. Box 151469, Arlington, Texas 76015; ©1986 through 1989 by Anthony D. Tooley; "Surface Forgiveness" (p.?).
8. Ibid.; illus. #553, "Put Away Malice".
9. 2 Cor. 5:17 NIV
10. A.R. Bernard (originally from Hans Urs von Balthasar)

Notes on Chapter 37: "Clothe Yourselves" (Col. 3:12 NIV)

1. Col. 3:12 NIV
2. Colossians & Philemon; Robert W. Wall; The IVP New Testament Commentary Series; Grant R. Osborne, series editor; Inter Varsity Press, P.O. Box 1400, Downers Grove, Ill. 60515; p. 145.
3. 1 Peter 2:9-10 NIV
4. Col. 3:12 NIV
5. INFO SEARCH; published by The Computer Assistant; P.O. Box 151469, Arlington, Texas 76015; ©1986 through 1989 by Anthony D. Tooley; "Kindness Builds Confidence".
6. How To Be a Christian in an UnChristian World; Fritz Ridenour; Regal Books (A Division of G/L Publications); Glendale, Calif. 91209; 1971; p. 133.

7. Philippians and Colossians; J. Vernon McGee; Thomas Nelson Publishers; Nashville, TN; 1991; p. 175.
8. 1 Peter 2:9 NIV

Notes on Chapter 38: "Put on Love" (Col. 3:14 NIV)

1. Col. 3:12a, 13a NIV (Italics mine)
2. Col. 3:13b NIV (Italics mine)
3. Illustrations for Biblical Preaching; edited by Michael P. Green; Baker Book House; Grand Rapids, Mich. 49516; ©1982, 1985, 189 by Michael P. Green; illus. #516; p. 152. "Forgiveness, Difficulty of".
4. INFO SEARCH; pub. by The Computer Assistant; P.O. Box 15149, Arlington, Texas 76015; ©1986 through 1989 by Anthony D. Tooley; illus. #818, "Simmer Down before Sundown!"
5. Encyclopedia of 7,700 Illustrations: Signs of the Times; Paul Lee Tan, ThD.; Assurance Publishers; P.O. Box 753, Rockville, Maryland 20851; ©1979 by Paul Lee Tan; illus. #1767, "Success on 'The Last Supper'"; pp. 457-458
6. Col. 3:13c NIV (Italics mine)
7. INFO SEARCH; op. cit.; illus. #1315, "Forgiving Like Christ".
8. Matt. 6:9-13 KJV
9. Matt 6:14-15 NIV
10. Col. 3:14a NIV
11. 1 Cor. 13:1-3 NIV
12. Col. 3:14 NIV
13. Studies in Colossians and Philemon; W.H. Griffith Thomas; Baker Book House; Grand Rapids, Michigan 49516; 1973; p. 114.

Notes on Chapter 39: "Let the Peace of Christ Rule in Your Hearts" (Col. 3:15a NIV)

1. Col. 3:15 NIV
2. Divine Comedy; Dante; Paradiso, Canto III, 85 (Italics mine)
3. The Faithful Christian: An anthology of Billy Graham; compiled by William Griffen & Ruth Graham Dienert; McCracken Press; 575 Madison Ave., Suite 1006, New York, NY 10022; 1994; pp. 143-144.

4. The Bible Exposition Commentary; vol. 2; Warren W. Wiersbe; Victor Books (A Division of Scripture Press Publications, Inc.) P.O. Box 1825, Wheaton, Illinois 60189; 1989; p. 139.
5. Col. 3:15a NIV (Italics mine)
6. The Letters to the Philippians, Colossians, and Thessalonians; The Daily Study Bible Series; rev. ed.; William Barclay; The Westminster Press; Philadelphia; 1975; p. 159.
7. Stefan Weaver, New Holland, PA.
8. Prov. 3:5-6 NIV
9. Isa. 26-3 NIV
10. Philippians 4:6-7 NIV
11. The Hiding Place; Corrie ten Boom with John and Elizabeth Sherrill; Guideposts Associates, Inc.; Carmel, NY 10512; ©1971 by Corrie ten Boom and John & Elizabeth Sherrill; pp. 66-67.
12. Col. 3:15a,b NIV
13. Col. 3:15c NIV
14. Illustrations for Biblical Preaching; ed. by Michael P. Green; Baker Book House; Grand Rapids, Michigan 49516; ©1982, 1985, 1989 by Michael P. Green; illus. #714, "Ingratitude", pp. 203-204.
15. Col. 3:15c NIV

Notes on Chapter 40: "With Gratitude" (Col. 3:16c NIV)

1. Knight's Up-to-the-Minute Illustrations. Walker B. Knight; Moody Press; Chicago; ©1974 by The Moody Institute of Chicago; "Spiritual Malnutrition", p. 22.
2. Col. 3:16a NIV
3. Ps. 119:11 NIV
4. From a story told in Meditation; Jim Downing; Nav Press; Colorado Springs, Colo; 1976; pp. 7-8.
5. Spiritual Intimacy; Richard Mayhue; Victor Books (A Division of Scripture Press Publications, Inc.) 1825 College Avenue, Wheaton, Ill. 60187; 1990; pp. 43-44.
6. Col. 3:16a NIV
7. Col. 3:16b NIV
8. Jn. 4:23 NIV
9. INFO SEARCH: published by The Computer Assistant; P.O. Box 151469, Arlington, Texas 76015; ©1986 through 1989 by Anthony D. Tooley; "Sing a New Song".

Notes on Chapter 41: "Do All in the Name of Jesus" (Col. 3:17b NIV)

1. Col. 3:17 NIV
2. Christian Clippings; 79 Pasco Rd., Wesley Chapel, FL 34249; Dec. 1974; Sermon by Rev. Dr. Donald Gilmore; pp. 7-8.
3. Jn. 17:3 NIV
4. Col. 3:11a NIV
5. The Bible Exposition Commentary; vol. 2; Warren W. Wiersbe; Victor Books (A Division of Scripture Press Publications, Inc.); P.O. Box 1825, Wheaton, Illinois 60189; 1989; p. 141.
6. Acts 4:7-10, 12 NIV
7. Philippians 2:9-11 NIV
8. Col. 3:17 NIV

Notes on Chapter 42: "Wives...Husbands" (Col. 3:18-19 NIV)

1. Col. 3:17 NIV
2. Crossing the Border: An expositional Study of Colossians; Guy H. King; Christian Literature Crusade; Fort Washington, PA; 1957; p. 97.
3. Col. 3:18 NIV
4. Colossians: Christ All-Sufficient; Everett F. Harrison; Moody Press; Chicago; ©1971 by the Moody Bible Institute of Chicago; p. 97.
5. The Letters to the Philippians, Colossians, and Thessalonians; The Daily Study Bible Series; rev. ed.; William Barclay; The Westminster Press; Philadelphia; 1975; pp. 160-161.
6. Proclaiming the New Testament; vol. 4; The Epistles to the Philippians, Colossians, and Philemon; Paul S. Rees; Baker Book House; Grand Rapids, Michigan; 1964; p. 104.
7. Gen. 2:21-22a NIV
8. Bible Illustrator; Parsons Technology, Inc.; One Parsons Drive, P.O. Box 100; Hiawatha, Iowa 52233-0100; ©1990-1992 by Parsons Technology, Inc.; Index 1627, "Husbands & Wives: Duty of Wives", p. 387.
9. Col. 3:19 NIV
10. Jn. 19:26-27

Notes on Chapter 43: "Children...Fathers" (Col. 3:20-21 NIV)

1. Article by Steve W. Butts, Senior Pastor of Millersville Bible Church; INFO SEARCH; published by The Computer Assistant; P.O. Box 151469, Arlington, Texas 76-15; ©1986 through 1989 by Anthony D. Tooley; #855, "How to be a Stupid Parent".
2. Col. 3:20 NIV
3. Exod. 20:12 NIV
4. Col. 3:21 NIV
5. The Letters to the Philippians, Colossians, and Thessalonians; The Daily Study Bible Series, rev. ed.; Wm. Barclay; The Westminster Press; Philadelphia; 1975; p. 163.
6. INFO SEARCH; op. cit.; "Declare Your Independence".
7. Deut. 4:4-7a NIV

Notes on Chapter 44: "It is the Lord Christ You are Serving" (Col. 3:24b NIV)

1. Col. 3:22 NIV
2. INFO SEARCH: published by The Computer Assistant; P.O. Box 151469, Arlington, Texas 76015; ©1986 through 1989 by Anthony D. Tooley; illus. #64, "A Thermometer or a Thermostat?"
3. Col. 3:23 NIV
4. INFO SEARCH; op. cit.; illus. #1141, "Give it Your Best!"
5. Col. 3:23 NIV
6. Sixty Fifth Annual Issue; Minister's Manual (Doran's); 1990 edition; edited by James W. Cox; Harper & Row Publishers; San Francisco; ©1989 by James W. Cox; "The Sacrament of Service," p. 1.
7. You are Loved & Forgiven: Paul's Letter of Hope to the Colossians; Lloyd John Ogilvie; Regal Books (A Division of GL Publications); Ventura, Calif., 1977; p. 189.
8. Col. 3:24 NIV
9. Crossing the Border: An Expositional Study of Colossians; Guy H. King; Christian Literature Crusade; Fort Washington, PA; 1957; p. 101.

Notes on Chapter 45: "you Have A Master in Heaven" (Col. 4:1 NIV)

1. Col. 3:25 NIV
2. Rom. 14:10b NIV
3. Gal. 6:7-8 NIV
4. Rom. 12:17-21 NIV
5. Bible Illustrator; Parsons Technology, Inc.; One Parsons Drive, P.O. Box 100, Hiawatha, Iowa 52233-0100; ©1990-1992 by Parsons Technology, Inc.; "Servants: Faithful", Index 603, p. 676.
6. Rev. 22:3-5 NIV
7. Col. 4:1 NIV
8. Treasures of Wisdom: Studies in Colossians & Philemon; Homer A. Kent, Jr.; BMH Books; Winona Lake, Indiana 49560; 1978; p. 131.
9. Colossians: The Church's Lord and the Christian's Liberty; Ralph P. Martin; Zondervan Publishing House, Grand Rapids, Michigan 49506; p. 132.
10. Philippians Colossians Philemon; Harlyn J. Kuschel; People's Bible Commentary; Concordia Publishing House; 3558 S. Jefferson Ave., St. Louis, MO 63118-3968; 1992; p. 191.
11. The Bible Exposition Commentary; vol. 2; Warren W. Wiersbe; Victor Books, A Division of Scripture Press Publications, Inc.; P.O. Box 1825, Wheaton, Illinois 60189; 1989; p. 145.
12. Col. 4:1 NIV
13. On Tiptoe with Joy; John T. Seamands; Baker Book House; Grand Rapids, Michigan; ©1967 by Beacon Hill Press of Kansas City; pp. 36-37.
14. Hymn "Make Me a Captive, Lord"; George Matheson; verse 1; 1890.

Notes on Chapter 46: "Devote Yourselves to Prayer" (Col. 4:2 NIV)

1. Col. 4:2 NIV
2. Tennyson; Morte D'Arthur; 1.415
3. INFO SEARCH; published by The Computer Assistant; P.O. Box 151469, Arlington, Texas 76015; ©1986 through 1989 by Anthony D. Tooley; #460, "Prevailing Prayer".
4. Acts 10:1-4 NIV

5. The Letters to the Philippians, Colossians, and Thessalonians; The Daily Study Bible Series, rev. ed.; William Barclay; The Westminster Press; Philadelphia; 1975; p. 166.
6. Col. 4:2b NIV
7. Col. 4:2 NIV

Notes on Chapter 47: "The Mystery of Christ" (Col. 4:3 NIV)

1. Col. 4:2-3a NIV
2. The Bible Exposition Commentary; vol. 2; Warren W. Wiersbe; Victor Books, A division of Scripture Press Publications, Inc.; P.O. Box 1825, Wheaton, Illinois 60-189; 1989; p. 146.
3. Col. 4:3a NIV
4. Acts 14:27 NIV
5. 2 Cor. 2:12 NIV
6. Rev. 3:8 NIV
7. Col. 4:3b NIV
8. Believers Church Bible Commentary; "Colossians, Philemon" by Ernest D. Martin; Herald Press; Scottdale, PA 15683; 1993; p. 198.
9. Jn. 3:16 NIV (Italics mine)
10. Gal. 3:28 NIV
11. Lamplighter (A semi-annual publication of Lancaster Bible College; 901 Eden Rd., Lancaster, PA 17601); Spring 1997; Gilbert A. Peterson, Ed. D.; editor-in-chief; "A Biblical Strategy for Friendship Evangelism", by Dr. Gordon H. Johnston.

Notes on Chapter 48: "Make the Most of Every Opportunity" (Col. 4:5b NIV)

1. Col. 4:5a NIV
2. New Courage for Daily Living: Devotions for Adults; Martin H. Franzmann; Concordia Publishing House; St. Louis, Missouri; 1963;p. 87.
3. Eph. 2:12-13 NIV
4. 2 Cor. 3:2-3 NIV
5. Col. 4:5b NIV
6. The Bible Exposition Commentary; vol. 2; Warren W. Wiersbe; Victor Books, A Division of Scripture Press Publications, Inc., P.O. Box 1825, Wheaton, Illinois 60189; 1989; p. 148.

7. Col. 4:6 NIV
8. 2 Timothy 2:23-24a NIV
9. INFO SEARCH; published by The Computer Assistant; P.O. Box 151469, Arlington, Texas 76015; 9/23/92; © by Anthony D. Tooley; illus #1090, "Try It, You'll Like It".
10. Ps. 34:4-8 NIV (Emphasis mine)

Notes on Chapter 49: "Fellow Servant" (Col. 4:7 NIV)

1. Col. 4:7a NIV
2. The Letters to the Philippians, Colossians, and Thessalonians; The Daily Study Bible Series; rev. ed.; William Barclay; The Westminster Press; Philadelphia; 1975; p. 169.
3. A New Approach to Colossians; L.J. Baggott; A.R. Mowbray & Co. Limited; London; 1961; p. 124.
4. Col. 4:7b NIV
5. 1 Cor. 4:2 NIV
6. Col. 4:7 NIV
7. Illustrations for Biblical Preaching; edited by Michael P. Green; Baker Book House; Grand Rapids, Michigan 49516; ©1982, 1985, 1989 by Michael P. Green; Illus. #1217, "Servanthood", p. 329.
8. The MacArthur New Testament Commentary: Colossians & Philemon; John MacArthur, Jr.; Moody Press; Chicago; 1992; p. 193.
9. Colossians and Philemon: The Supremacy of Christ; R. Kent Hughes; Crossway Books; Westchester, Ill. 60154 (A Division of Good News Publishers); ©1989 by R. Kent Hughes; p. 144.
10. Col. 4:8 NIV
11. Hymn "O Master, Let Me Walk with thee"; Washington Gladden; 1879; vss. 1, 2 & 4.

Notes on Chapter 50: "Onesimus" (Col.. 4:9 NIV)

1. Col. 4:9a NIV
2. Colossians and Philemon: The Supremacy of Christ; R. Kent Hughes; Crossway Books; Westchester, Illinois 60154 (A Division of Good News Publishers); ©1989 by R. Kent Hughes; p. 145.
3. Philemon 10-12 NIV

4. The Men, the Meaning, the Message of the New Testament Books; William Barclay; The Westminster Press; Philadelphia; ©1976 by Wm. Barclay; p. 89.
5. Ibid.; p. 90.
6. Philemon 18-19a NIV
9. Barclay; op. cit.; p. 88.
10. Luke 10:35
11. Philemon 19b, 21 NIV
12. According to St. Paul: A Study Course on the New Testament Letters; H.F. Mathews; The Macmillan Company; New York; 1957; p. 84
13. Col. 4:9a NIV
14. Col. 4:9b NIV
15. Studies in Colossians and Philemon; W.H. Griffith Thomas; Baker Book House; Grand Rapids, Michigan 49516; 1973; p. 132.
16. Paul and the Intellectuals: The Epistle to the Colossians; A.T. Rojbertson; rev. ed. by W.C. Strickland; Broadman Press; Nashville, TN (1956?); p. 135.
17. Isa. 40:8 NIV

Notes on Chapter 51: "Welcome Him" (Col. 4:10c NIV)

1. Col. 4:10a NIV
2. The New Testament Message: A Biblical-Theological Commentary; Wilfrid Harrington, O.P. & Donald Senior, editors; vol. 15: "Colossians" by Patrick V. Rogers, C.P.; Michael Glazier, Inc.; 1210A King Street, Wilmington, Delaware 1980; p. 85.
3. The MacArthur New Testament Commentary: Colossians & Philemon; John MacArthru, Jr.; Moody Press; Chicago; 1992; p. 194.
4. You are Loved & Forgiven: Paul's Letter to the Colossians; Lloyd John Ogilvie; Regal Books (A Division of GL Publications); Ventura, California; 1977; p. 273.
5. Illustrations for Biblical Preaching; ed. by Michael P. Green; Baker Book House; Grand Rapids, Michigan 49516; ©1982, 1985, 1989 by Michael P. Green; illus. #214, p. 72.
6. Col. 4:10b NIV
7. Mk. 14:51-52 NIV

8. Men with a Message: An Introduction to the New Testament and its Writers; John Stott (revised by Stephen Motyer); William B. Eerdmans Publishing Company; 255 Jefferson Ave., S.E., Grand Rapids, Michigan 49503; 1994; p. 16.
9. Acts 13:5
10. Acts 13:13 NIV
11. Studies in Colossians and Philemon; W.H. Griffith Thomas; Baker Book House; Grand Rapids, Michigan 49516; edited by Winifred G.T. Gillespie; 1973; p. 133.
12. Colossians and Philemon: The Supremacy of Christ; R. Kent Hughes; Crossway Books; (A Division of Good News Publishers); Westchester, Illinois 60154; © by R. Kent Hughes 1989; p. 150.
13. Acts 15:36-39a NIV
14. Col. 4:10 NIV
15. The Letters to the Philippians, Colossians, and Thessalonians; The Daily Study Bible Series; rev. ed.; William Barclay; The Westminster Press; Philadelphia; 1975; p. 170.
16. 2 Timothy 4:11 NIV
17. Matt. 10:8b NIV

Notes on Chapter 52: "They Have Proved a Comfort to Me" (Col. 4:11b NIV)

1. Col. 4:11a NIV
2. The Letters to the Philippians, Colossians, and Thessalonians; The Daily Study Bible Series; rev. ed.; William Barclay; The Westminster Press; Philadelphia; 1975; p. 170.
3. Treasures of Wisdom: Studies in Colossians & Philemon; Homer A. Kent, Jr.; BMH Books; Winona Lake, Indiana 49560; 1978; p. 143.
4. 1 Cor. 1:26-29 NIV
5. Col. 4:11b NIV
6. Ernest D. Martin; op. cit.; p. 212.
7. Col. 4:11 b, c NIV
8. Exodus 18:13-18, 21-22 NIV
9. Illustrations for Biblical Preaching; edited by Michael P. Green; Baker Book House; Grand Rapids, Michigan 49516; ©1982, 1985, 1989 by Michael P. Green; issue. #207, p. 70.
10. Ps. 137:1, 4 NIV

11. Ezek. 3:15 NIV

Notes on Chapter 53: "Mature" (Col. 4:12 NIV)

1. Col. 4:12a NIV
2. The Expositor's Bible Commentary; Frank E. Gaebelein, General Editor; vol. 11 (Ephesians-Philemon); "Colossians" by Curtis Vaughan; Regency Reference Library, Zondervan Publishing House; 1415 Lake Drive S.E., Grand Rapids; Mich. 49506; 1978; p. 224.
3. 2 Cor. 5:15 NIV
4. Col. 4:12b NIV
5. Living on the Mountain: Strength and Encouragement from God's Daily Care; Roger C. Palms; Fleming H. Revell Company; Old Tappan, NJ 07675; ©1977, 1986 by Roger C. Palms.
6. Col. 4:12b NIV
7. Ibid.
8. The Divine Comedy; Paradiso; canto 3, 1.85; Dante Alighierl.

Notes on Chapter 54: "Give My Greetings" (Col. 4:15a NIV)

1. The New Testament: It's History and Theology; James L. Price; Macmillan Publishing Company; 866 Third Avenue, New York, NY 10022; ©1987 by Macmillan Publishing Company.
2. Treasures of Wisdom: Studies in Colossians & Philemon; Homer A. Kent, Jr. BMH Books; Winona Lake, Indiana 49560; 1978; p. 147.
3. Col. 4:13
4. Knight's Treasury of Illustrations; Walter B. Knight; Wm. B. Eerdmans Publishing Company; Grand Rapids, Michigan 49503; ©1963 by Wm. B. Eerdmans Publishing Company; Rev. T.W. Gallaway, D.D; p. 376.
5. Col. 4:14
6. The MacArthur New Testament Commentary: Colossians & Philemon; John MacArthur, Jr.; Moody Press; Chicago; 1992; pp. 197-198.
7. Col. 4:14 NIV
8. 2 Tim. 4:9-10a NIV

9. Crossing the Border: An Expositional Study of Colossians; Guy H. King; Christian Literature Crusade; Fort Washington, PA; 1957; pp. 132-133.
10 John 6:66-68 NIV
11. Col. 4:15 NIV
12. Studies in Colossians: The Pre-Eminent Christ; Richard Sturz; Moody Press; Chicago; 1955; p. 125.

Notes on Chapter 55: "See That it is Read" (Col. 4:16 NIV)

1. Col. 4:16a NIV
2;. The Bible Exposition Commentary; vol. 2; Warren W. Wiersbe; Victor Books, A. Division of Scripture Press Publications, Inc.; P.O. Box 1825, Wheaton, Ill 60189; 1989; p. 153.
3. Col. 4:16bNIV
4. According to St. Paul: A Study-course on the New Testament Letters; M.F. Matthews; The Macmillan Company; New York; 1957; p. 74.
5. Isa. 55:112 NIV
6. Col. 4:17 NIV
7. Philemon 2 NIV
8. Lectures on the Epistle to the Colossians; H.A. Ironside; Loizeaux Brothers, Publishers; 1 East 13th St., New York, N.Y.; 1928; pp. 184-185.
9. Col. 4:17 NIV
10. Rom. 14:7-8 NIV
11. Bible Illustrator; Parsons Technology, Inc.; One Parsons Drive, P.O. Box 100, Hiawatha, Iowa 52233-0100; ©1990-1992 by Parsons Technology, Inc.; p. 149, Topic: Consecration; Title: The Faithful Fragrance, index; 35-8-3511.

Notes on Chapter 56: "Grace be with You" (Col. 4:18 NIV)

1. Col. 4:18a NIV
2. When God Whispers Your Name; Max Lucado; Word Publishing; Dallas, TX; ©1994 by Max Lucado; pp. 30-31.
3. Col. 4:18a NIV
4. Treasures of Wisdom: Studies in Colossians & Philemon; Homer A. Kent, Jr.; BMH Books; Winona Lake, Indiana 49560; 1978; p. 149.

5. Rom. 16:22 NIV
6. Col. 4:18b NIV
7. The Letters to the Philippians, Colossians, and Thessalonians; The Daily Study Bible Series; rev. ed.; William Barclay; The Westminster Press; Philadelphia; 1975; p. 175.
8. Lk. 14:27-30 NIV
9. Col. 418c NIV
10. Acts & Paul's Letters; vol. 7; Interpreter's Concise Commentary; edited by Charles M. Laymon; "The Letter of Paul to the Colossians" by Victor Paul Furnish; Abingdon Press, Nashville, TN; 1983; ©1971 & 1983 by Abingdon Press; p. 393.
11. Rev. 22:21 NIV (Emphasis mine)
12. The Letter to the Colossians; T.J. Barling; published by "The Christadelphian"; 404 Shaftmoor Lane, Birmingham B28 8 S2; 1972; p. 181.
13. Hymn "Amazing Grace"; John Newton (1779) (Paired with a 19th century American melody); vss 1-3.
14. Let the Redeemed of the Lord Say So! by H. Eddie Fox and George E. Morris; Abingdon Press; Nashville, TN; 1991; pp. 171-172.

Other inspiring titles from Higher Ground Books & Media:

Full Gospel by Rev. Jerry C. Crossley

Shine Like Stars by Rev. Jerry C. Crossley

Holy Ways in Holidays by Rev. Jerry C. Crossley

The Seen and The Unseen by Rev. Jerry C. Crossley

Journey to Jesus by Rev. Jerry C. Crossley

It's Only a Game by Darrel Johnson

Our Journey of Faith by Miranda Thornsberry

One Step(pe) at a Time by Lori (Martin) Potts Zimmerman

Revealing His Might and Power by Deanna Rodriguez

The Children's Bread by Terra Kern

Music and the Holy Spirit by Stephen Shepherd

Breaking the Cycle by Willie Deeanjlo White

Shameless Persistence by Sandra Bretting

Wise Up to Rise Up by Rebecca Benston

Soul Solutions by Terri Kozlowski

Add these titles to your collection today!

http://www.highergroundbooksandmedia.com

HIGHER GROUND BOOKS & MEDIA IS AN INDEPENDENT PUBLISHER

Do you have a story to tell?

Higher Ground Books & Media is an independent Christian-based publisher specializing in stories of triumph! Our purpose is to empower, inspire, and educate through the sharing of personal experiences. We are always looking for great, new stories to add to our collection. If you're looking for a publisher, get in touch with us today!

Please be sure to visit our website for our submission guidelines.

http://www.highergroundbooksandmedia.com/submission-guidelines

HGBM SERVICES IS OUR CONSULTING FIRM

AUTHOR SERVICES

HGBM Services offers a variety of writing and coaching services for aspiring authors! We can help with editing, manuscript critiques, self-publishing, and much more! Get in touch today to see how we can help you make your dream of becoming an author a reality!

*****

We also offer social media marketing services for authors, small businesses, and non-profit organizations. Let us help you get the word out about your book, your projects, and your mission. We offer great rates, quality promos, consistent communication, and a personal touch!

http://www.highergroundbooksandmedia.com/editing-writing-services

Need Bulk Copies?

If you would like to order bulk copies of this book or any other title at Higher Ground Books & Media, please contact us at highergroundbooksandmedia@gmail.com.

We offer discounts for purchases of 20 or more copies. Excellent for small groups, book clubs, classrooms, etc.

Get in touch today and get a set of great stories for your students or group members.